The Musée d'Orsay

The Musée d'Orsay

Ministère de le Culture et de la Communication
Editions de la Réunion des musées nationaux

Thames and Hudson
Paris 1987

Translated from the French by Jane Brenton

Frontispiece: Mercié's David *(ill. 15),*
with the former station clock in the background

ISBN 2-7118-2.049-1 (French edition, RMN, November 1986)
ISBN 2-7118-2.110-2 (English edition, RMN)

Layout: Massin

Printed and bound in West Germany by Mohndruck, Gütersloh

Contents

*The Musée d'Orsay from the
right bank of the Seine*

Introduction

Paris has acquired a new museum, the Musée d'Orsay, just across the river from the Louvre.

Inevitably the question will be asked, what possible need is there for another museum in a city already so richly endowed? What will it offer to the public that cannot be seen elsewhere? What will be different about it? How will its displays be presented? In attempting to answer these questions I shall touch briefly on the events that led up to the decision to found a new cultural centre, and explain the general purpose it is intended to serve, before moving on to a conducted tour of the museum galleries.

To anyone who has visited the Jeu de Paume in recent years it must be obvious that the building was far too small. Situated in the Tuileries gardens, with a beautifully light and open aspect, it was the ideal home for the Louvre's collections of Impressionist painting when it first opened in 1947. Thirty years later this was demonstrably no longer the case. The building could not do justice to a collection swollen by numerous bequests and acquisitions. Nor, given the universal appeal of Impressionism, could it safely accommodate the visitors who arrived each year in increasing numbers. It was clear that more space was urgently needed, the more so as the collection received a massive injection of new works in 1977 as a direct consequence of the transfer of the Musée National d'Art Moderne from the Palais de Tokyo to its new home in the Pompidou Centre. All the Post-Impressionist paintings belonging to the Musée National d'Art Moderne (the Pont-Aven School and the Neo-Impressionists), together with numerous late nineteenth-century works by French and foreign artists (largely Naturalist and Symbolist in character, and inherited for the most part from the former Musée du Luxembourg) at that time reverted effectively to the Louvre. This was in no way exceptional, since it had always been the practice, at periodic intervals, to remove paintings, sculptures and drawings that could no longer be regarded as representative of 'modern' art from the Luxembourg to the Louvre. Thus it was always envisaged that the Post-Impressionist works temporarily displayed at the Palais de Tokyo from 1978 onwards would one day be reunited with the Impressionists: it was obviously desirable for Signac and Cross to be seen with Seurat, and Bernard and Sérusier with their close associate, Gauguin.

One possible solution might have been to extend the Jeu de Paume itself. But that would still not have provided the necessary space, and especially not in the light of recent interpretative developments. In one of those radical shifts in perspective that from time to time breathe new life into the history of art and aesthetics, a 'new' nineteenth century has begun to emerge, one that is far less of an orderly linear progression than the doctrinaire critics of the past had contemplated. First came the memorable exhibition 'Sources du XXe siècle' (Paris, 1960), which established Art Nouveau fairly and squarely as one of the major movements that have enriched and altered the course of twentieth-century Western art. Then, in the ensuing years, there have been reappraisals of Symbolism in its various manifestations, of industrial and 'Beaux-Arts' architecture, of Second Empire eclecticism, of photography and even of 'academic' sculpture, for so long utterly dismissed and derided. In addition, certain schools of European and American painting, hitherto somewhat eclipsed in France by the brilliance of Paris, have now, happily, come to be viewed in a more impartial light.

Of course it would be foolish to deny that, in some respects, this new interpretation is still open to debate: there is a certain cultural snobbery and speculative self-interest attached to espousing the latest fashionable ideas, and we cannot be certain that all these newly regarded artists are in fact neglected geniuses. Nevertheless, over the last twenty years a persuasive case has been made, in a series of stimulating books, articles and exhibitions, for a radical reappraisal of nineteenth-century art history, and there is no possible way in which an enlarged Jeu de Paume could have given expression to that broader perspective.

The primary need was for space – and a lot of it. That space was found in the Gare d'Orsay, a vast and virtually disused railway station right in the heart of Paris, in the immediate vicinity of the Louvre and the Tuileries.

The idea of establishing a museum of late nineteenth-century art in the Gare d'Orsay building dates back to 1973, when a proposal put forward by the Direction des Musées de France was approved in principle by the government of President Georges Pompidou. The station was already threatened with demolition to make way for the construction of a vast hotel, and railway traffic had been reduced to a few suburban services. The immediate effect of the decision was that the building itself was rescued. Long regarded as a *fin-de-siècle* monstrosity, it profited from the revival of interest in the nineteenth century, an aesthetic about-turn that unfortunately came too late to save Louis-Pierre Baltard's central market buildings, Les Halles,

demolished in 1973. The Orsay plan was approved and set in motion by President Valéry Giscard d'Estaing, and a civil commission was formed in 1978 to supervise the scheme, to which his successor François Mitterrand pledged his full support in 1981. Thus the long and necessarily difficult enterprise of setting up a new museum was made possible by the active championship of three French presidents.

If the museum breaks new ground in terms of its contents – its intended scope, the collections themselves – so it does in terms of its context, the adaptation of an existing building (the station and its adjacent hotel) to a new function as a multi-disciplinary museum.

First, a few words about the contents. As a national museum, the Musée d'Orsay is the repository of the state collections of the art of the second half of the nineteenth century and the early years of the twentieth. It therefore stands between the Louvre, the home of the national collections for the years preceding 1850, and the Musée National d'Art Moderne, which has charge of works dating from after 1905–10 (those, with a few exceptions, of artists born after 1870).

It is perhaps worth mentioning at this point that the dates chosen – 1848–50 on the one hand, and 1905–10 on the other – were arrived at only after careful consideration and debate. Various other possibilities were discussed for the starting date: any earlier, moving back into the Romantic period, would have required a much bigger museum altogether; any later, say 1863–65, and the date would have had little meaning except in the narrow context of French painting. It was finally decided that the mid-point of the century most accurately corresponded to changes taking place over the whole spectrum of activity, and not only in the political or social sphere. The emergence of Courbet and Millet at the Salons of 1848 and 1850, the foundation of the Pre-Raphaelite Brotherhood in 1848, the erection of Joseph Paxton's Crystal Palace (1850–51) and of the new Louvre (started in 1852), were all in their different ways indications of a change in sensibility – as, at the other end of the scale, was the radical break marked by Picasso's *Les Demoiselles d'Avignon* of 1907.

Dealing with a period that is particularly rich and prolific, the museum aims to reflect that diversity by looking beyond painting, sculpture and the decorative and graphic arts (drawing, print-making and photography) to give an account of developments in the other visual arts: architecture, town-planning and film – a turn-of-the-century invention – as well as other processes for the dissemination of images: posters, the press, book illustrations. In addition, a number of small 'dossier' exhibitions on individual themes, as well as films and audio-visual displays, will bring out the relationships between the visual arts and other contemporary forms of artistic expression (such as literature and music, represented at the museum by a programme of concerts), and serve to situate developments across the spectrum in a historical context.

Adopting a multi-disciplinary approach, unlike the Louvre or the permanent installations of the Musée National d'Art Moderne, the museum faced certain problems from the outset. If such an ambitious scheme was to be translated into practice, if all the spheres of artistic activity and all the various techniques were to be properly represented, then clearly the existing resources of the national collections (the paintings, sculptures and rare *objets d'art* in the Louvre, the Jeu de Paume and the Palais de Tokyo) would not suffice. It was necessary to enlist the co-operation of other museums and organizations (Versailles, Fontainebleau, Compiègne; the Musée des Arts Décoratifs; the state furniture collection (Mobilier National); the Sèvres porcelain factory), which agreed to contribute a number of major items. Where possible, state-owned paintings and sculptures were recalled from provincial museums and other works were offered in exchange. Above all, herculean efforts were made to increase existing stocks. The Musée d'Orsay is indebted in this respect to its many benefactors, among them the newly formed Society of Friends of the Museum; it has also been the beneficiary of a number of major bequests, offset against payment of death duties; and it has itself pursued an active purchasing policy, with the aid of special grants. For the most part the need was to remedy the more glaring omissions in the existing collections, while that was still possible, but in some areas it was necessary to start from scratch, notably with *objets d'art*, furniture, architecture and photography. In respect of prints and engravings, however, it was decided not to establish new collections, but to represent the various print-making techniques (including poster art and book illustration) by borrowing on a regular basis from the Bibliothèque Nationale, the principal repository of the national collections in these branches of the graphic arts. Drawings (apart from pastels and architectural drawings housed in the Musée d'Orsay) would similarly remain in the nearby Cabinet des Dessins in the

Louvre, readily available for display in a changing series of exhibitions.

Can we therefore claim that the museum offers a comprehensive panorama of art in the second half of the nineteenth century? Indeed not. Many major artists will be missing, especially foreigners. There are entire movements, schools and techniques that are unrepresented, or dealt with inadequately. But, within those limitations, we have endeavoured to take into account the sheer versatility of creative expression within the period and to show how the different strands of activity are interwoven. We have not attempted to create an artificially balanced view. The accidents of the art market, the preferences of a particular collector or the generosity of a painter's descendants will sometimes have caused one artist to figure more prominently than another of equal importance. That is no bad thing. A museum should not be like an encyclopaedia that gives a strictly objective and impersonal account: it must inevitably reflect the tastes, the choices – and also the blind spots and oversights – of the collectors, connoisseurs and curators who over the years have built up the collections.

There will be plenty of time in the future for discussion of the image of the nineteenth century presented by the Musée d'Orsay, and for that image to be expanded and refined.

Let us now pass on to the building that provides the context for the exhibitions, the Gare d'Orsay and the adjoining Hôtel d'Orsay, designed by Victor Laloux and built on the site of the former Cour des Comptes, destroyed by fire in 1871. The whole structure was put up in under two years, and was opened on 14 July 1900 as part of the World Fair celebrations. It was a

The ruins of the former Cour des Comptes (Palais d'Orsay), burnt down in 1871

supremely functional design, with the trains running on the lower level, while all the peripheral activities associated with ticket offices, waiting-rooms and left-luggage offices, etc., were grouped together on the upper level, beneath the monumental vaulted roof. The station was enclosed on two sides by the four

1er Juillet 1900

The Gare d'Orsay shortly before its opening in 1900

hundred bedrooms and reception rooms of a luxury hotel, its stone façades concealing the metal structures within and vying in grandeur with the great palaces that line the Seine.

There was much to be done to adapt this dinosaur of the railway age to its new function: within its volume, spaces had to be created that were capable of housing permanent displays and temporary exhibitions, as well as entrance halls, storerooms, workshops and rooms for the various services; the best possible lighting conditions had to be ensured for the different categories of exhibits, and an efficient system of access devised for visitors; at the same time the identity

of Laloux's original building needed to be preserved. This was the challenge that confronted the architects who entered the competition held in 1979.

The winning design was submitted by ACT (R. Bardon, P. Colboc, J. P. Philippon), who were joined in 1980 by the Italian architect Gae Aulenti, winner of a second competition for the interior design and museum layout. The solution they have provided is bold and imaginative. The vaulted roof space of the 'Nave' is kept open and undisturbed; within it is a new structure consisting of a central avenue (following the alignment of the old railway lines) on either side of which are ranged exhibition rooms surmounted by terraces. These rooms and terraces communicate on two levels with rooms in the entrance hall suite, adjacent to the Nave and looking out over the Seine. In the roof space, at the top of the station and hotel, are a series of airy galleries with natural overhead lighting. The elaborately decorated reception rooms on the first floor of the hotel are integrated with the rest of the museum as exhibition areas, and the hotel dining-room becomes the museum restaurant.

Thus the exhibition space is divided into three main levels, linked by stairways and escalators situated at either end of the building.

As we have said, the design is bold and uncompromising. At no point is there any use of pastiche, nor has any attempt been made to create a stylistic harmony between the new structure and the old. Laloux's stucco décor has been respected; the cast-iron pillars and beams (including those in hitherto inaccessible parts of the station, in the roof space and on the upper levels) have been restored and given new prominence. The new architecture, while itself making a strong series of geometric statements in metal and stone, never masks the presence of the original building.

Internal coherence is supplied by the use of the same materials and colours throughout (Burgundy stone, light-coloured partitions, dark brown or blue metalwork, etc.). But within that overall unity the rooms are clearly differentiated, a variety of architectural solutions being employed to ensure the optimum conditions for the different types of display.

The design perfectly complements the range and diversity of the artefacts and activities to be accommodated within the museum. In planning the layout of the exhibition space, it was felt essential to create a number of distinctly demarcated areas, both for the sake of clarity and to reduce the displays to a manageable scale. On a purely practical level, it was important to keep separate the educational facilities ('dossiers' and theme exhibitions, reference rooms, audio-visual displays) and the galleries themselves, which needed an atmosphere of peace and quiet. Generally it was desirable to make a distinction between the different media and techniques, while taking care to avoid arbitrary groupings with no basis in historical truth. And, finally, the physical layout had to reflect the differences and antagonisms between opposing schools and aesthetic tendencies: thus it was decided to show in quite separate areas of the museum, on the one hand the development of Impressionism (after 1870) and of Post-Impressionism, and on the other the various alternative strands which evolved over the same period, and which in the past have been dismissed wholesale as the work of 'official hacks' or *pompiers*.

The Galerie Bellechasse

The collections, then, are displayed on three levels, in a series of 'sequences' clearly differentiated by their individual architectural settings and by their contents.

The visitor begins on the first level with a brief historical introduction (films and displays of objects designed to illustrate some aspect of history or society in the latter half of the nineteenth century), and thereafter the ground floor is devoted exclusively to the period 1848–75. The central avenue is lined with monumental sculpture from Rude to Carpeaux; the row of rooms on one side is devoted to a sequence on Realism up to the beginnings of Impressionism; that on the other side to the inheritance of Romanticism (Delacroix) and of Neoclassicism (Ingres), culminating in eclecticism and Symbolism. Eclecticism is most fully represented in the section on the decorative arts and finds its apotheosis in the Opéra room, which pays tribute both to Charles Garnier's great building and to the performances presented there. On the same level are a number of areas set aside for temporary exhibitions of drawings, engravings and photographs, and for 'dossiers', thematic displays relating to the period 1848–75.

To reach the second level, which is right at the top of the building, the visitor can either ascend via the escalators at the end of the central hall, or can make his or her way up through the exhibition rooms of the Pavillon Amont, the station's 'upstream' or western pavilion, devoted to permanent and temporary displays on the theme of architecture and town-planning.

This topmost level contains the longest sequence of works in the museum, being set aside exclusively for Impressionism after 1870 and the various movements that developed in its wake (Neo-Impressionism, the Pont-Aven School, the Nabis, etc). On the same level is a cafeteria and an audio-visual display area, as well as space for exhibitions of the graphic arts.

The route down from the second to the third level (situated on the middle floor) leads past a number of documentary exhibitions on the press, poster art and book illustration, and also the historical reference facilities in the Galerie des Dates.

The third and last stage of the tour begins in the former reception rooms of the hotel, which contain examples of official art and the large-scale decorative works of the Third Republic. The visitor then re-enters the open spaces of the Nave. The terraces set above the central avenue show the sculpture of the last third of the century, dominated by Rodin, and ending with Maillol and Bourdelle in the early years of the twentieth century. The first group of rooms opening off the terraces is devoted to Naturalism, Symbolism and academic art at the end of the century. There then follows the great sequence of Art Nouveau (France and Belgium), with an extension in two towers erected at the end of the central hall, and in adjacent rooms devoted to the architects and designers of

Glasgow, Vienna and Chicago. Space has been left for 'dossier' exhibitions for the period 1870–1910, and the history of painting is brought to a conclusion with a selection showing, on the one hand, the development afer 1900 of the former Nabis (Bonnard, Vuillard, etc.), and on the other, the new directions in painting of the years 1904–06 (Matisse, the Fauves), as an introduction to the art of the twentieth century. The visit ends with a final sequence – and here the word is particularly apt – on the invention of cinematography.

Michel Laclotte
Inspecteur Général des Musées

Note on the captions

Where no medium is given, the work is in oil on canvas.
Dimensions are given in centimetres and inches.
For paintings, height is given before width;
for sculpture, height only;
for *objets d'art*, height, width
and depth (height only for chairs).

The text of this book is the work of the following contributors:
Valérie Bajou, Marc Bascou, Françoise Cachin, Anne Distel,
Claire Frèches, Chantal Martinet, Françoise Heilbrun,
Geneviève Lacambre, Ségolène Le Men, Antoinette Le Normand Romain,
Henri Loyrette, Philippe Néagu, Jean-Michel Nectoux,
Sylvie Patin, Anne Pingeot, Nicole Savy,
Philippe Thiébaut, Georges Vigne.

1

2

Sculpture:
the last Romantics

Although Romanticism began to influence painting in the 1820s, it was not until ten years later that the first Romantic sculptures appeared.

Taking their inspiration from Dante, Shakespeare or Chateaubriand, rather than from ancient history, they were intended to be both faithful copies of nature and eloquent expressions of feeling. Antoine Préault (1809–79) exaggerated forms, proportions and modelling. 'Shout louder' was François Rude's exhortation to his wife as she posed for his *Génie de la Patrie* (*Spirit of Patriotism*) – which was immediately christened 'the shrew in a rage'. Bitterly attacked by the academic critics, these artists found themselves gradually excluded from the Salons during the July Monarchy of King Louis-Philippe (1830–48). Without commissions they were hard put to survive, and had no means of bringing themselves to the public's attention except through publications and the press. In 1847, Rude (1784–1855) executed for a certain Captain Noisot a monument symbolizing that officer's affection and loyalty for his Emperor, whom he had served as Commander of the Grenadiers on the island of Elba, but it was not until the Second Empire that the state gave any sign of official approval. Préault's medallions of Dante and Vergil were acquired by Napoleon III in 1853. Jean-Baptiste Carpeaux (1827–75) found himself in serious trouble at the French school in Rome (the Villa Médicis) over his *Ugolin* (*Ugolino*), which represented all that the Institut de France in its role as guardian of the classical tradition most deplored; but state commissions were issued to Jean-Bernard Duseigneur (1809–66) in 1867 for a cast of *Roland furieux* (*Orlando Furioso*) and to Préault for a cast of his *Ophélie* (*Ophelia*) in 1876. It should however be noted that the plaster casts of these works dated from 1831 and 1842 respectively!

'I stand not for the finite, but for the infinite' was Préault's inscription on his medallion of Delacroix, now in the Louvre. It is a phrase that neatly encapsulates the spirit of the times, which was to find its fullest expression in the Symbolism of Auguste Rodin who, noted Camille Mauclair, was loved by the poets of his day 'because he makes the most finite of the arts suggest infinity'.

1 *F. Rude:* Napoléon s'éveillant à l'immortalité (Napoleon awakening to Immortality), *1846 Plaster. 225 (88.6). Acquired 1891. The bronze is at Fixin (Côte-d'Or)*

2 *A. Préault:* Ophélie (Ophelia) *Plaster executed in 1842. 75 × 200 (29.5 × 78.7). Acquired and cast in bronze 1876*

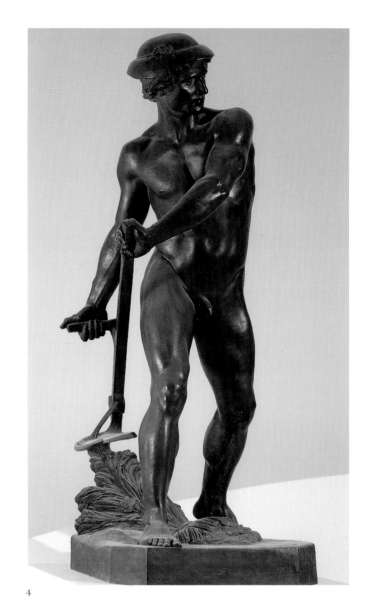

4

3

5

Painting:
Ingres, Delacroix,
Chassériau after 1850

At the beginning of the Second Empire (1852–70) the artistic scene was dominated by two great figures: Jean-Auguste-Dominique Ingres (1780–1867) and Eugène Delacroix (1798–1863). The former, the champion of classical art, won the Prix de Rome in 1801 and was elected a member of the Institut de France in 1825; the latter, the leading exponent of Romanticism, was obliged to wait until 1857 before finally being admitted to that august body. Both were appointed to the imperial commission responsible for the Paris World Fair of 1855, the only painters on the committee. This was the first such occasion to include an international retrospective of painting; this was housed in a Palais des Beaux-Arts, constructed especially on the avenue Montaigne. A vast temporary display of the art of the first fifty years of the century, it gave Ingres and Delacroix the ideal opportunity to show some of their best work. Ingres's *La Source* (*The Spring*), a reworking of an earlier study, was not completed until 1856, and was then exhibited in the artist's studio before being put on show by its new owner, Count Duchâtel, in a special room 'surrounded by large plants and aquatic flowers, so that the Nymph of the Spring will look even more like a real person'. This 'adolescent Eve', harking back to an 'incalculable antiquity' according to some observers, was to Gustave Moreau an '"academy" (in the antique style) ... executed by a marvellous scholar'. *La Source* is the most famous example of the fashion for smooth-textured painting, practised not only by the pupils of Ingres, such as Hippolyte Flandrin (1809–64) or Amaury-Duval (1808–85), but also by Léon Bénouville (1821–59) and other pupils of François Picot (1786–1868), and by students of Charles Gleyre (1806–74), such as Jean-Louis Gérôme (1824–1904). The latter, at the age of only twenty-two, painted a picture which attracted attention at the 1847 Salon and became famous under the title of *Un Combat de coqs* (*A Cockfight*), a free interpretation of a classical theme.

Delacroix's technique could hardly have provided a greater contrast. It was much admired by Charles Baudelaire, who called it 'a veritable explosion of colour'. This description of the ambitious canvas *La chasse aux lions* (*The Lion Hunt*), commissioned for the Musée de Bordeaux and

3 *G. J. Thomas:* Virgile (Vergil), *1859–61 Marble. 183 (72). Commissioned 1859, entered national collection 1874*

4 *E. Guillaume:* Le faucheur (The Reaper), *1849–55 Bronze. 168 (66.1). Acquired 1855*

5 *E. Cavelier:* Cornélie, mère des Gracques (Cornelia, Mother of the Gracchi), *1861 Marble. 171 (67.3). Acquired 1861*

6 *J. A. D. Ingres:* La Source
(The Spring)
*163 × 80 (64.2 × 31.5). Started
in Florence c. 1820, completed
in Paris 1856 with the aid of
Paul Balze and Alexandre
Desgoffe. Bequest of Comtesse
Duchâtel, 1878*

7 *E. Delacroix:* La chasse aux
lions (The Lion Hunt), *1854
86 × 115 (33.9 × 45.3). Sketch
for the painting commissioned
by Musée de Bordeaux and
shown at Paris World Fair
1855. Acquired 1984*

7

8

8 *T. Chassériau:*
Tépidarium; salle où les
femmes de Pompéi venaient
se reposer et se sécher en
sortant du bain (Tepidarium:
Room where the Women of
Pompeii Rested and Dried
Themselves on Leaving the
Bath)
*171 × 258 (67.3 × 101.6). Salon
of 1853. Acquired 1853*

9

10

exhibited in 1855, applies even more aptly to the large, impassioned sketch for it in the Musée d'Orsay, referred to in Delacroix's diary for 3 May 1854: 'In the morning, fired with enthusiasm, went on with the sketch for *The Lion Hunt*.' Featured in all the Delacroix retrospectives, including the posthumous exhibition of 1874, this sketch must inevitably have had an influence on painters like Manet, Renoir, Signac and Matisse.

In his lifetime, too, Delacroix had his adherents, among them Théodore Chassériau (1819–56), formerly a pupil of Ingres. He was a portraitist and also a painter of goddesses and nymphs, biblical and oriental scenes, and decorative works for churches and public buildings. In the course of his brief career – he was only thirty-seven when he died – he won praise from critics and public alike, because he seemed to bring together 'the two rival schools of drawing and of colour'. The *Tépidarium*, acclaimed at the Salon of 1853, is a case in point: the setting is carefully modelled on Pompeian antiquity, but Chassériau brings his women to life, their languorous poses reminiscent of Delacroix's exotic harem scenes. The half-size figures place Chassériau outside the monumentalist traditions of history painting. The *Tépidarium* was in fact one of the first examples of the historical *genre* painting which achieved dominance under the Second Empire.

Although the tour of the Musée d'Orsay opens with a tribute to Ingres and Delacroix, showing how their late paintings relate to the works of subsequent painters, it is perhaps worth reiterating that – like Corot, who is also represented in the Musée d'Orsay – they were born in the eighteenth century: the main body of their work remains in the Louvre.

9 *Amaury-Duval:* Madame de Loynes *(1837–1908), 1862* *100 × 83 (39.4 × 32.7). Bequest of Jules Lemaître, 1914*

10 *J. L. Gérôme:* Jeunes grecs faisant battre des coqs *ou* Un combat de coqs (Young Greeks Holding a Cock Fight), *1846* *143 × 204 (56.3 × 80.3). Salon of 1847. Acquired 1873*

11 *A. Falguière:* Vainqueur
au combat de coqs (Winner at
the Cock Fight). *Bronze. 174
(68.5). Salon of 1864. Acquired
1864*

Sculpture: eclecticism

11

12 *P. Dubois:* Chanteur
florentin (Florentine Singer),
*1865. Silvered bronze. 155 (61).
Commissioned 1865 and
shown at Paris World Fair
1867*

13 *A. E. Carrier-Belleuse:*
Hébé (Hebe), *1869. Marble.
207 (81.5). Entered national
collection 1869*

14 *H. Moulin:* Trouvaille à
Pompéi (A Find at Pompeii),
*1863. Bronze. 187 (73.6).
Acquired 1864*

French society was transformed by the industrial revolution
that took place during the Second Empire. Fortunes changed
hands, and the newly affluent bourgeosie set about creating
its own style. Needing confirmation of their status, its
members tended to look to the past to provide models.
Historical subjects were the fashion in the nineteenth
century; writers, and later artists, scoured earlier civilizations
for themes they could adapt to their own purposes. Such
evidence of culture and good taste was warmly received by
their new patrons.

The Hellenistic bronzes of Pompeii, and Giovanni da
Bologna's *Mercury*, were the inspiration to Alexandre
Falguière (1831–1900) and Hippolyte Moulin (1832–84) for
their figures of athletic young men, exhibited at the Salon of
1864. Together with Paul Dubois and Antonin Mercié, these
two sculptors formed a group known as Les Florentins, in
acknowledgment of their debt to Tuscany. Many of the
drawings of Dubois (1829–1905) were based on works by
Benozzo Gozzoli. Dubois' *Petit chanteur du XVème siècle*
(*Florentine Singer*) won the gold medal at the Salon of 1865,
arousing such enthusiasm that a quarrel broke out between
the Emperor's cousin Princess Mathilde and the Director of

12

13

14

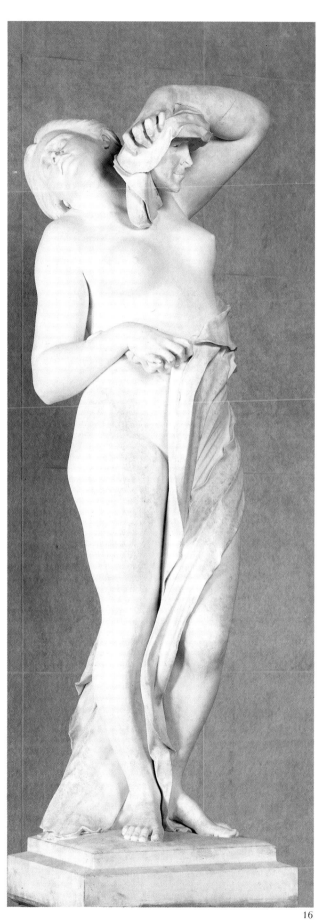

15

16

15 *A. Mercié:* David, *1872–73*
Bronze. 184 (72.4). Assigned to
national collection 1874

16 *E. Christophe:* La
Comédie humaine *ou* Le
masque (The Human
Comedy *or* The Mask),
1857–76
Marble. 245 (96.5). Acquired
1876

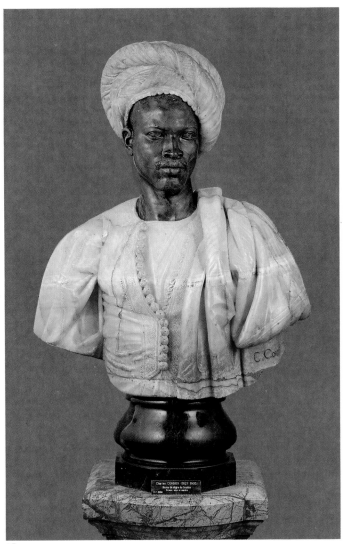

17

17 *C. Cordier:* Nègre du
Soudan (Sudanese Negro),
1857
Bronze and onyx. 96 (37.8)
overall. Acquired 1857

the Beaux-Arts, Count Nieuwerkerke, as to who should have
the first cast; it was the Princess who emerged victorious.
Small replicas of the figure were produced both in bronze
(Barbedienne) and in unglazed porcelain (Sèvres). Mercié
(1845–1916), while still technically a student in residence at
the Villa Médicis in Rome, was awarded the Légion
d'Honneur for his second-year work, a *David* sheathing his
sword, a superbly flowing and developed human figure.

Albert-Ernest Carrier-Belleuse (1824–87) also used a
classical model for his finest relief, *Hébé et l'aigle* (*Hebe and
the Eagle*). *The Comédie humaine* (*The Human Comedy*) by
Ernest Christophe (1827–92) inspired Baudelaire's thoughts
on the 'correspondences' between poetry and sculpture, in
Chant XXI of *Les Fleurs du mal* of 1857.

Love of history in this period was matched by a taste for
far-off places. Charles Cordier (1827–1905) obtained funding
for a series of expeditions, the most tangible result of which
was the lavish use, in his sculpture, of onyx mined in the
newly opened Algerian quarries. The employment of rich,
coloured stone in statuary was then much in vogue, reflecting
the affluence of the age.

Painting: eclecticism

The huge canvas by Thomas Couture (1815–79), *Romains de la décadence* (*Romans of the Decadence*), commissioned in 1846 and exhibited at the Salon of 1847, is based on a quotation from one of Juvenal's satires: 'More cruel than war, vice battened on Rome and avenged the conquered world.' The composition draws on established formal models, and there are clear references to Tiepolo, Rubens, Poussin and, in particular, Veronese. However, it is interesting that Couture had no hesitation in showing his figures in unheroic poses. This was in marked contrast to the idealism of those artists who exactly conformed to what they were taught at the Ecole des Beaux-Arts, where the ultimate reward, for winners of the Prix de Rome, was a period of residence in Italy at the Villa Médicis. Among such prize-winners were Alexandre Cabanel (1823–89), honoured in 1845; William Bouguereau (1825–1905) and Paul Baudry (1826–86), in 1850; Elie Delaunay (1821–91), in 1856; and Henri Regnault

18 *T. Couture:* Romains de la décadence (Romans of the Decadence)
466 × 775 (183.5 × 305.1).
Salon of 1847. Acquired 1847

19 *A. Cabanel:* Naissance de
Vénus (Birth of Venus)
*130 × 225 (51.2 × 88.6). Salon
of 1863. Acquired by Napoleon
III 1863, assigned to national
collection 1879*

(1843–71), in 1866. Success at this early stage was the
guarantee of a brilliant career. Thus in 1863, already the
recipient of a Salon medal, Cabanel was elected to the Institut
de France and made a professor at the Ecole des Beaux-Arts.
In the same year he had enormous success at the Salon with
his *Naissance de Vénus* (*Birth of Venus*), which was immediately bought by Napoleon III for his private collection.

Cabanel's pupil, Regnault, was unusual in that he spent
only two years in Italy before moving on to Spain. All official
residents of the Villa Médicis were obliged to make regular
submissions of their work. Regnault sent his fourth-year
work from Tangiers: *Exécution sans jugement sous les rois
maures de Grenade* (*Summary Execution under the Moorish
Kings of Granada*). Such was the youthful painter's fame that
his death in battle at Buzenval in 1871 shocked the artistic
world.

20 *H. Regnault:* Exécution
sans jugement sous les rois
maures de Grenade
(Summary Execution under
the Moorish Kings of
Granada), *1870*
302 × 146 (118.9 × 57.5).
Acquired 1872

21

21 *E. Delaunay:* Peste à
Rome (Plague in Rome)
131 × 176.5 (51.6 × 69.5).
Based on the legend of St
Sebastian in the Golden
Legend *of Jacobus de*
Voragine. Salon of 1869.
Acquired 1869

One of the finest examples of Second Empire history
painting is Delaunay's *Peste à Rome* (*Plague in Rome*),
exhibited at the Salon of 1869. The canvas was the
culmination of many years of work. Life drawings were made
for every single figure, and there are numerous smaller
versions and preparatory studies which reveal how the
composition developed in dramatic intensity, moving towards the isolation of the central group of exterminating
angels.

Decorative arts: eclecticism

Eclecticism embodies the belief that all styles are equal. This was an emergent trend in the mid nineteenth century, and corresponded to the aspirations of a rising bourgeoisie, who looked to the past or to the colonial experience for their models. As industry and commerce boomed, so the stylistic blend gained an international currency. The World Fairs, with their exhibitions of artefacts from many different countries, prompted a realization of the dire consequences of over-rapid industrialization, and a number of ventures were started which aimed to reconcile Utility with Beauty. Design schools, societies for the promotion of design, and museums of applied arts were established; competitions and special exhibitions were held, and reviews and pattern-books were published. Eclecticism was a source of creative regeneration, since it encouraged designers to measure themselves against the geniuses of antiquity, to take as their standard the very best that history and the contemporary world could offer: it also fostered a revival of interest in nature. Hence commercial designers show a variety of stylistic emphases within a framework of Naturalism: Sevin (Neoclassical); Avisseau and Frullini (Neo-Renaissance); Schilt and Cremer (Neo-Rococo); Deck (Islamic); Braquemond and Rousseau (Japanese), to name but a few.

The big industrial firms hired the best designers – architects, sculptors, painters and above all ornamentalists – whose industrial work was exhibited and won awards. What these artists had in common, in spite of their apparent diversity of style, was a desire to think on a large scale, a concern for quality, a superb audacity in the way they juxtaposed motifs or used unusual combinations of materials and colours, and an enthusiasm for new scientific ideas. As well as one-off pieces commissioned by individual patrons or destined for international exhibitions, there began to appear works designed with mass-production in mind, quickly produced and available to a wider public. At the other end of the spectrum, the traditions of craftsmanship were maintained by a small number of producers who rejected mechanization and the division of labour.

22 *A. L. Barye, sculptor:* Clock with Chariot of Apollo *Bronze with green patina, red marble. 85 × 94 × 36 (33.5 × 37 × 14.2). From a mantelpiece garniture originally including two candelabra, commissioned by Isaac Pereire for the Château d'Armainvilliers in 1858. Loaned by Ministère des Affaires étrangères*

23

24

25

23 *F. D. Froment-Meurice, goldsmith; J. F. Duban, architect; A. V. Geoffroy-Dechaume, sculptor; J. J. Feuchère, sculptor; M. Liénard, ornamentalist:* Jewel casket, one of a pair *Silver, parcel-gilt, painted enamel, emeralds and garnets. 42.6 × 35.8 × 27.5 (16.8 × 14.1 × 10.8). Exposition nationale des produits de l'Industrie, Paris, 1849. From a dressing-table set commissioned for the wedding of the Duchess of Parma, grand-daughter of Charles X, in November 1845, completed only in 1851. Acquired 1981*

24 *C. J. Avisseau, ceramicist; O. Guillaume de Rochebrune, designer and engraver:* Cup and stand *Faïence with coloured relief and inlaid decoration. Cup 34.5, d. 26.5 (13.6, d. 10.4). Stand 8, d. 51.5 (3.1, d. 20.3). World Fair, Paris, 1855. In reaction against the rise of industrially produced ceramics, Avisseau revived pottery as an art form, inspired by the work of Bernard Palissy. Acquired 1983*

25 *Fourdinois, company founded by Alexandre Georges Fourdinois in 1835 and managed from 1867 by Henri-Auguste Fourdinois:* Neo-Renaissance cabinet *Carved walnut, jasper and lapis-lazuli. 253 × 143 × 60 (99.6 × 56.3 × 23.6). World Fair, Paris 1867. Musée des Arts Décoratifs*

26 *C. G. Diehl, cabinet-maker; E. Brandely, designer; E. Fremiet, sculptor:* Medal cabinet *Cedar, walnut, ebony and ivory, with silvered bronze and (galvanized?) copper. 238 × 151 × 60 (93.7 × 59.4 × 23.6). World Fairs, Paris 1867 and Vienna 1873. Acquired 1973. Fremiet's plaster for the central relief,* Entrée triomphale de Mérovée à Châlons-sur-Marne (The Triumphal Entry of Merovaeus into Châlons-sur-Marne), *was given by Madame René Martin in 1973*

27

28

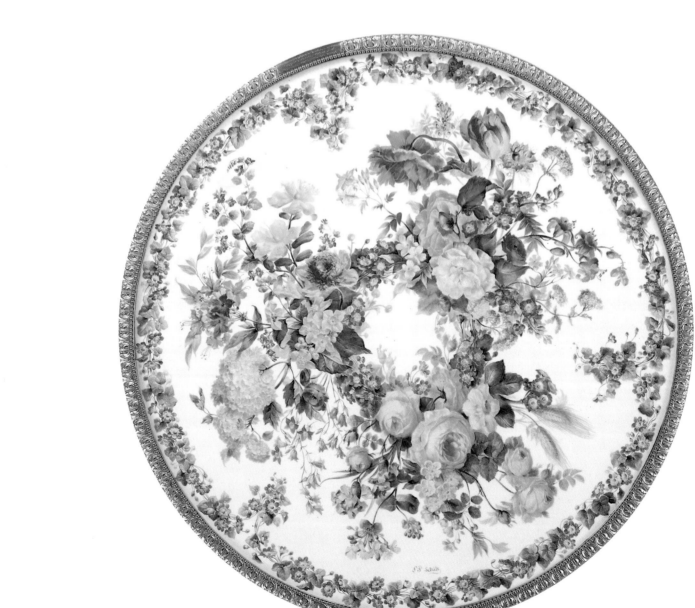

36
29

27 Manufacture de Creil et
Montereau: F. Bracquemond,
painter and engraver;
E. Rousseau, ceramicist and
glassmaker: Table centrepiece
Faïence with printed and
painted underglaze decoration.
15 × 62 × 42
(5.9 × 24.4 × 16.5). World
Fair, Paris 1867. Part of the
'Japanese' dinner service
commissioned from
Bracquemond by Rousseau in
1866, manufactured by
Leveille up to 1903. Acquired
1984

28 E. Rousseau, ceramicist
and glassmaker: Vase
bambou. Bamboo vase.
Engraved and enamelled
glass. 28 (11). World Fair,
Paris 1878. Acquired 1984

29 Sèvres, Manufacture
Impériale de Céramique:
Guéridon (Tray), 1850–53
Porcelain with painted
decoration, incised and gilded
bronze. D. 87 (34.3). Presented
to Duchess of Hamilton by
Empress Eugénie, 1853.
Acquired 1982.

30

30 Christofle et Cie, company
managed by H. Bouilhet and
P. Christofle; A. E. Reiber,
designer: Candelabrum, one
of a pair
Patinated and gilt bronze,
cloisonné enamel. 56 (22). Part
of a set originally including a
flower-stand, executed for the
Vienna World Fair, 1873.
Acquired 1982

31 E. Lièvre, designer;
E. Detaille, painter: Cupboard
on supporting table
Rosewood, gilt bronze,
engraved ironwork.
211 × 111 × 57
(83.1 × 43.7 × 22.4). Probably
manufactured by L'Escalier
de Cristal, as was a similar
piece decorated with a
painting of a Japanese woman
by Clairin (Hermitage
Museum, Leningrad).
Acquired 1981

Arts and Crafts

A. W. N. Pugin (1812–52), whose principles of honest, functional architecture were derived from a study of Gothic art, sowed the seeds for the Arts and Crafts Movement that grew up in England from the 1860s onwards as a reaction against the dehumanizing effects of mechanization. Thomas Carlyle and John Ruskin, while condemning the way men were being taken over by machines, did not allow their moral indignation to sway their essentially reactionary view of society. Others such as Robert Owen (the father of English Socialism), Henry Cole (organizer of the first World Fair, the Great Exhibition of 1851, and one of the pioneers of industrial design) and, above all, William Morris, adopted a more pragmatic approach.

It is to Morris (1834–96) that the credit goes for translating theory into practice. In 1861 he set up his own firm and devised a system of production that integrated craftwork with mechanization, making it possible to produce both everyday household articles and luxury goods. Morris attracted many imitators and disciples: some, such as Arthur Heygate Mackmurdo (founder of the Century Guild, 1882), Walter Crane (Art Workers' Guild, 1884), Charles Robert

34

Ashbee (Guild of Handicraft, 1888) and Ernest Gimson (Kenton and Co., 1890), ultimately foundered on the contradictions inherent in the Arts and Crafts Movement, which tended to create luxury craft items beyond the pockets of all but the prosperous few.

Others, among them Edward William Godwin (1833–86) and Christopher Dresser (1834–1904), chose to work in association with industrial concerns; strongly influenced by Japanese design, they developed a stripped-down Anglo-Japanese style that was ideally suited to mass-production.

Almost all these designers had a background in architecture, and in some instances practical experience of the profession; it was this as much as anything that gave them their vision of a harmonious art of living that would be available, theoretically at least, to all.

34 *Morris & Co., London; W. Morris, painter and designer:* Painted wood panelling, detail *100 × 1200 (39.4 × 472.4) overall. From the home of the Earl of Carlisle, Palace Green, London. The decor of the dining-room also included paintings by Burne-Jones:* Cupid and Psyche *(City Art Gallery, Birmingham). Acquired 1979*

35

Puvis de Chavannes, Moreau, Degas

Pierre Puvis de Chavannes and Gustave Moreau were both admirers, as young men, of the vast decorative works executed by Chassériau between 1844 and 1848 for the stairway of the Cour des Comptes. (These suffered war-damage in 1871 and were removed in 1898, shortly before the building was demolished to make way for the Gare d'Orsay; today they are in the Louvre.)

Decoration is a strong element in the work of Puvis de Chavannes (1824–98), whether or not a painting was conceived with a particular location in mind. His *Eté* (*Summer*) could not be described as a naturalistic depiction of agricultural activity, nor is it precisely an allegory. In the words of the critic Georges Lafenestre, who saw the picture exhibited at the Salon of 1873, where it was acquired for the nation: 'This is not summer in Beauce or Brie. It is summer in an eternal land which the artist's soul inhabits; feelings there are no less intense, but they are more generalized.'

It is precisely this quality of timelessness, allied to a rejection of chiaroscuro in favour of pale, clear colours and flattened, simplified design, that made his work so attractive to the Symbolist painters of the latter years of the century, and in particular to Gauguin, Maillol and the Nabis. *Le pauvre pêcheur* (*The Poor Fisherman*), of 1881, was initially greeted with mild puzzlement, before being hailed as the 'ultimate emblem of poverty' (*synthèse de la misère*) when it entered the Musée du Luxembourg in 1887.

Like Puvis de Chavannes, Edgar Degas (1834–1917) abandoned his law studies in order to concentrate on painting and, also like him, travelled in Italy, where some of his relations lived. It was during a visit to Florence, in 1858, to see his aunt Laure Bellelli (née De Gas – it was the painter himself who adopted the form Degas) that he started *La famille Bellelli* (*The Bellelli Family*). This ambitious composition draws on the tradition of the posed family photograph. Even more strikingly, it echoes the style of Ingres, for whom Degas had a profound admiration. The final canvas was preceded by numerous sketches, drawn and painted, both of details and of the whole picture. The work was discovered in the artist's studio after his death and was acquired for the

35 *P. Puvis de Chavannes:* L'Eté (Summer) *305 × 507 (120 × 199.6). Salon of 1873. Acquired 1873 for Musée de Chartres and assigned to national collection 1986*

36 *P. Puvis de Chavannes:* Le
pauvre pêcheur (The Poor
Fisherman), *1881*
*155 × 192.5 (61 × 75.8). Salon
of 1881. Acquired 1887*

national museums when the contents were put up for auction. The painting demonstrates Degas' consummate skill in portraiture, as alert to details of contemporary life as to the psychology of his sitters. A number of other portraits of his family and friends are also to be seen in the Musée d'Orsay.

In the early years of his career Degas aspired to the status of a history painter, as witness his *Sémiramis construisant Babylone* (*Semiramis Building Babylon*) of 1861; although this particular canvas was not exhibited at the Salon, it is typical of the series of history compositions exhibited by the young painter in the 1860s.

The Degas of these early years has many points of similarity with Gustave Moreau (1826–98), with whom he became friendly in 1859. Moreau was a pupil of Picot and knew Chassériau well. From 1864 onwards he was hugely successful at the Salon: the Musée d'Orsay has in its possession his *Jason*, from the Salon of 1865, and the *Orphée* (*Orpheus*) shown there in 1866. The latter was selected for permanent exhibition in the Musée du Luxembourg, and was regarded at the time as a masterpiece worthy of the Renaissance. The iconographic invention of the young Thracian girl reverently bearing the head and lyre of the bard slain by the Maenads marks one of the first appearances of a theme used widely by the Symbolists in the second half of the nineteenth century, to represent the artist (Orpheus or John the Baptist) whose ideas and creations live on beyond his death.

37 *E. Degas:* Sémiramis contruisant Babylone (Semiramis Building Babylon), *1861* *151 × 258 (59.4 × 101.6).* *Acquired 1918*

38

38 *E. Degas:* Portrait de
famille; la famille Bellelli
(The Bellelli Family). *Baron
G. Bellelli, his wife, née Laure
De Gas, the artist's aunt, and
their daughters
200 × 250 (78.7 × 98.4). Started
in Florence, 1858, and perhaps
exhibited at the Salon of 1867.
Acquired 1918, with assistance
from Comte and Comtesse de
Fels, by kind agreement of
René De Gas*

39 *G. Moreau:* Orphée
(Orpheus), *1866*
*154 × 99.5 (60.6 × 39.2). Salon
of 1866. Acquired 1866*

39

Aspects of painting
outside France

Until the very end of the nineteenth century, few serious efforts were made to secure works by foreign painters for the contemporary collection of the Musée du Luxembourg (one of the exceptions being Oswald Achenbach, during the Second Empire). If non-French painters were represented, it was usually because they were resident in France. No one thought to take advantage of the unique opportunity presented by the World Fairs, with their international art exhibitions, and when the idea surfaced in 1900 it was already too late to do much about it.

In 1915, Edmund Davis donated his collection of English painting, and an annexe was opened at the Jeu de Paume, in 1922, specifically for foreign works. Even so, the museum had

40 *A. Böcklin:* La chasse de Diane (Diana the Huntress), *1896*
100 × 200 (39.4 × 78.7).
Acquired 1977

40

41

42

46

no major painting by Sir Edward Burne-Jones (1833–98) until that deficiency was remedied recently by the acquisition of *The Wheel of Fortune* – which was, in fact, one of the artist's own favourite works: Puvis de Chavannes had tried unsuccessfully to have it included in one of the first Salons of the Société Nationale des Beaux-Arts, of which he was then President. Burne-Jones, associated with the second 'romantic' phase of Pre-Raphaelitism, reveals in this picture a debt to Michelangelo, Mantegna and Botticelli, whose works he studied in the course of his last trips to Italy, in 1871 and 1873, and who were to have a profound influence on the paintings of his maturity.

Hans Makart (1840–84) was a highly respected painter in his native Austria, and his reputation spread to France at the time of the World Fair of 1878. His vast compositions attempt to make history painting into something immediate and enthralling; exuberant swirls of Baroque forms, they are full of echoes of Rubens. Makart was also well known as a decorator, and his two large compositions of *Abundantia* were originally destined to grace the dining-room of the Palais Hoyos in Vienna.

The Swiss painter Arnold Böcklin (1827–1901) had little contact with France, preferring to travel in German-speaking countries and visiting Italy on several occasions. Elements of Symbolism begin to appear in his work from around 1870 onwards. His landscapes, whether calm or stormy, have a peculiar atmospheric quality that suggests the forces of nature at work; the mythological figures he introduces are no more than a confirmation of the stated theme. *La chasse de Diane* (*Diana the Huntress*) is a reworking of a theme treated thirty years before, and still betrays its original classical influences.

41 *E. Burne-Jones:* The Wheel of Fortune, *1877–83* *200 × 100 (78.7 × 39.4).* *Acquired 1980*

42 *H. Makart:* Abundantia: les dons de la terre (Abundantia: the Fruits of the Earth), *1870* *162 × 447 (63.8 × 176).* *Acquired 1973*

43 *H. Makart:* Abundantia: les dons de la mer (Abundantia: the Fruits of the Sea), *1870* *163 × 448 (64.2 × 176.4).* *Acquired 1973*

43

Carpeaux

44 *J. B. Carpeaux:* Napoleon
III, c. *1864*
Terracotta. 17.5 (6.9). Gift of
Jacques Doucet, 1908

45 *J. B. Carpeaux:* Le prince
impérial et son chien Néro
(The Prince Imperial and his
Dog Nero), *1865*
Marble. 140 (55.1). Gift of
Jacques Doucet, 1908

46 *J. B. Carpeaux:*
L'impératrice Eugénie et le
prince impérial (Empress
Eugénie and the Prince
Imperial)
Terracotta. 26 (10.2). Gift of
Jacques Doucet, 1908

47 *J. B. Carpeaux:* Ugolin
(Ugolino)
Bronze. 194 (76.4).
Commissioned 1862. Salon of
1863

'A statue conceived by the poet of the *Divine Comedy* and
created by the begetter of Moses: that would indeed be a
masterpiece of the human spirit', wrote Jean-Baptiste Carpeaux (1827–75) in 1854, the year in which he won the Prix
de Rome at his tenth attempt. Carpeaux is of course referring
to Dante and Michelangelo, who were revered by the
sculptors of the latter half of the nineteenth century and were
the direct inspiration for his own *Ugolin* (*Ugolino*). This piece
was originally conceived as Carpeaux's official submission in
his final year of residence at the Villa Médicis, and, although
it did not conform to the rules laid down by the Académie de
France in Rome, was recognized as a masterpiece by Count
Nieuwerkerke, himself a sculptor. Through him, Carpeaux
was introduced to the Imperial court, and though not the
official portraitist (a post held by Jean-Auguste Barre) he
produced a number of vivid terracottas of Napoleon III and
the Empress. His sole official commission was for a full-
length marble statue of the Prince Imperial with his dog. The
three figures shown here give an indication of Carpeaux's
talents – qualities of observation and lively expression –
which are equally apparent in his paintings.

Naturally enough, the major public commissions were
reserved for winners of the Prix de Rome – and there was no
lack of new façades to decorate in the Second Empire.
Carpeaux sculpted the allegorical figure of *La France*
impériale protégeant l'Agriculture et les Sciences (*Imperial*
France protecting Agriculture and the Sciences) to crown the

44

45

46

53

54 Model of the Opéra stage
*App. 160 (63). Executed for
the Paris World Fair, 1900.
Loaned by Musée de l'Opéra
and Bibliothèque de l'Opéra*

55 *C. Garnier:* The New
Paris Opéra, longitudinal
section
*Engraving. 47 × 74
(18.5 × 29.7). Published by
Ducher et Cie, Paris, 1878*

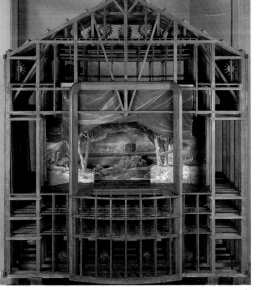

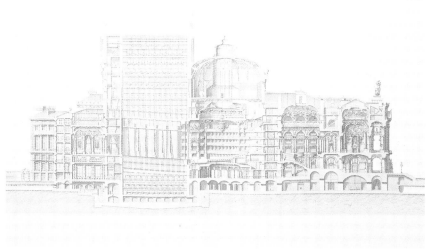

54

55

57

58

59

60

Daumier

Although during his lifetime Honoré Daumier (1808–79) was renowned chiefly for his caricatures and lithographs, the twentieth-century public is equally appreciative of the paintings and sculptures that he often used as points of departure. The Musée d'Orsay is fortunate in possessing virtually all Daumier's major sculptures. The *Emigrants* and *Ratapoil* have long been in the state collections, and thanks to the generosity of Monsieur Michel David-Weill, these were joined in 1980 by the original series of thirty-six painted clay busts of *Parlementaires* (*Parliamentarians*). Begun in 1832, these caricature-portraits of prominent political figures show how Daumier made use of the general vogue for caricature and turned it into a political weapon. He did not rely on anecdote but on piercingly exact observation and wonderfully expressive draughtsmanship and modelling. His bold distortions seem to reveal the inner nature of his subjects, at the same time distinguishing them as clearly identifiable human types. It is this very modern aspect of his work that sets him apart from the Romantics of his generation and justifies the decision to show his sculpture at the Musée d'Orsay rather than in the Louvre.

57–60 H. Daumier: Dr C. Prunelle *(1774–1863), parliamentarian (57);* Ch. Philipon *(1800– 62), journalist (58);* J. C. Fulchiron *(1774–1859), poet and parliamentarian (59);* F. Guizot *(1787–1874), interior minister (60) Coloured unfired clay. 31 (12.2); 16 (6.3); 17 (6.7); 22 (8.7). Commissioned by Philipon as models for lithographs published 1832–35 in his periodicals* Le Charivari *and* La Caricature. *Acquired 1980 with assistance from Michel David-Weill and the Lutèce Foundation*

61 H. Daumier: Les émigrants (The Emigrants), *first version, c. 1848–50 Plaster. 31 × 67.5 (12.2 × 26.6). Acquired 1960*

56 H. Daumier: La blanchisseuse (The Washerwoman) *49 × 33.5 (19.3 × 13.2). Acquired 1927 with assistance from D. David-Weill*

62

63

56

Millet

The scenes of peasant life that made Jean-François Millet (1814–75) famous in the 1880s were regarded in his lifetime as subversive. Under the Second Empire not a single one of his canvases was acquired for the Musée du Luxembourg, although two paintings were purchased shortly after Millet's death – *L'église de Gréville* (*The Church at Gréville*) and a small early picture of *Baigneuses* (*Bathers*). However, largely thanks to the generosity of individual collectors, the Louvre has been able to build up over the years a remarkable collection of his work. His *Le printemps* (*Spring*) was donated in 1887 by the widow of Frédéric Hartmann, who com-

missioned from Millet a set of *Four Seasons* – never in fact completed. The canvas is a fine example of the painter's late manner. Beautifully lit and with wonderfully clear colours, it is not so much a landscape as the expression of a dialogue between nature, shaped by man, and man himself, a tiny figure under a menacing sky; the symbolism of the season is reinforced by the choice of a morning setting.

Millet's characteristic brand of Naturalism consists in this ability to evoke a precise instant while yet investing it with a universal significance. The most famous example of his work is *L'Angélus* (*The Angelus*), which came to the Louvre as part of a major bequest by Alfred Chauchard in 1909. He acquired it in 1890 from the American Art Association, which had taken the picture on a triumphant tour of the American cities after buying it, only a year before, at the Secretan sale of 1 July 1889.

Des glaneuses (*Gleaners*) passed to the Louvre in 1890. This major work had attracted bitter criticism when first exhibited at the Salon of 1857. In an age when it was believed that poverty had been eradicated, the painting seemed to conjure up the spectre of revolution. Paul de Saint-Victor wrote in *La Presse*: 'While Monsieur Courbet is tidying up and adjusting his style, Monsieur Millet is becoming more entrenched in his. His three *Gleaners* have immoderate pretensions; they pose like the Three Fates of Pauperism. They are scarecrows in rags.' Millet's cause was, however, taken up by one critic, Jules Castagnary, who sensed the emergence of a new style that would replace the exhausted genre of history painting. Castagnary chose therefore to find a parallel with the classical past, describing the canvas as 'one of those great and true passages such as Homer and Vergil lighted upon'. The comparison is not inapt: the gleaners recall the sculptures of the Parthenon. Their massive weight is an essential part of their power of expression.

The Barbizon School; late Corot

Millet went to live at Barbizon in 1849, and continued to paint scenes of peasant life, looking to the village itself or the Chailly plain for his subject matter rather than the nearby forest of Fontainebleau itself. That great area of woodland had for some twenty years been a favourite spot for artists, who arrived in their numbers to paint and draw from nature. One of these was Millet's friend Théodore Rousseau (1812–67), who had suffered many rejections at the hands of the academic jury under Louis-Philippe, and began to receive official recognition only after 1848, in the Second Republic. A perfectionist, he reworked his paintings obsessively and made it a rule to paint always from the motif – as for example in the forest landscape pierced by a vertical shaft of sunlight, exhibited at the Salon of 1849 as *Une avenue* (*An avenue*), which he painted in the spring of 1846 while staying with the landscapist Jules Dupré at L'Isle-Adam.

Narcisse Diaz de la Peña (1807–76) started out as a painter of amorous interludes and fantasies in a Romantic spirit, and by 1860 was successful enough to enjoy an extravagant lifestyle. After meeting Théodore Rousseau in 1837, he returned regularly to Fontainebleau and became perhaps the most skilled of all the group at conveying the effects of light on the trees and undergrowth. The critic Thoré noted that Diaz's supremacy lay in 'the quality of the colour, which is

65 *T. Rousseau:* Une avenue, forêt de L'Isle-Adam (An Avenue in the Forest of L'Isle-Adam)
101 × 82 (39.8 × 32.3). Salon of 1849. Bequest of Alfred Chauchard, 1909

66 *N. Diaz de la Peña:* Les hauteurs du Jean de Paris (forêt de Fontainebleau) (The Jean de Paris Heights, Forest of Fontainebleau), *1867*
84 × 106 (33.1 × 41.7). Bequest of Alfred Chauchard, 1909

65

66

67 *J. B. C. Corot:* L'atelier de
Corot. Jeune femme à la
mandoline (Corot's Studio.
Young Woman with
Mandolin), c. *1865–70*
56 × 46 (22 × 18.1). Acquired
1933

68 *J. B. C. Corot:* Une
matinée. La danse des
nymphes (Morning. The
Dance of the Nymphs)
98 × 131 (38.6 × 51.6). Salon of
1850–51. Acquired 1851

67

always determined by the light', and that 'his pictures resemble a mound of precious stones'. His technique almost certainly influenced Monticelli and Renoir, to whom he gave advice and encouragement.

Rousseau and Diaz have close ties with Romanticism and, like Delacroix, are represented in the Musée d'Orsay only by a few works of particular significance (notably those from the Chauchard collection; see p. 65). The rest of their work is to be seen in the Louvre.

Another major painter whose works are mainly in the Louvre, but who is represented in the Musée d'Orsay collections, is Jean-Baptiste Camille Corot (1796–1875), born in the eighteenth century but active well into the nineteenth. His career was unsensational, but he was greatly esteemed by the younger painters and by the more perspicacious of the critics, among them Charles Baudelaire who admired his technique and 'unfailingly strict harmonies'.

Corot travelled in Italy, stayed at Barbizon, and ranged the length and breadth of France, from Brittany to Dauphiné. To make his work acceptable to the academic Salon jury, he felt obliged to introduce historical and mythological figures into landscapes that otherwise would have been rejected as little more than sketches. It was the increasing respectability of Naturalism in the Second Empire that presented him with the freedom to pursue his own inclinations, encouraged too, no doubt, by the expansion in demand from private patrons.

At about this time his manner became more lyrical and he began to paint misty evocations of nature (well represented in the Chauchard collection). *La danse des nymphes* (*The Dance of the Nymphs*) is typical; it was exhibited at the Salon of 1850–51 and purchased by the state for the Musée du Luxembourg, where it was put on show in 1854 – the only painting by Corot to be given that official stamp of approval during his lifetime.

Less well-known, and largely dismissed by his contemporaries, is Corot's painting of individual figures, posed either outdoors or in studio interiors, and dressed in exotic disguises or theatrical costumes. Corot treated these works as exercises in pure painting, anticipating Cezanne's fundamental explorations of technique. Although he also painted portraits of friends and relatives, for studies of this type Corot preferred to employ professional models, not wishing to be distracted by individual personality. The melancholy of the attitude of the pensive young woman in *L'atelier* (*The Studio*) is tempered by the play of light on her dress and face, and on the tapestry of the chair to the left; there is a discreet symbolism in the objects about her, the landscape on the easel making a reference to painting and the mandolin suggesting a tune left unfinished.

75 *G. Courbet:* La falaise
d'Etretat après l'orage (The
Cliff at Etretat after the
Storm)
*133 × 162 (52.4 × 63.8). Salon
of 1870. Presented by Office
des biens privés, 1950*

75

canvases had been included. In the event the Pavillon du
Réalisme, with an exhibition of forty of his paintings, was not
a success; only his friends praised the venture, among them
the critic Champfleury, generous enough to overlook the
portrait of himself in *The Painter in his Studio*, which he
disliked intensely.

Courbet's two major compositions did not enter the
national collections until many years later: the *Burial at
Ornans* was presented to the Louvre to coincide with an
exhibition held at the Ecole des Beaux-Arts in 1882,
'Exposition des oeuvres de G. Courbet', marking the artist's
long-delayed official recognition, and the *Studio* remained in
private hands until 1920.

Apart from these paintings, which shocked the Second
Empire public and were satirized by the cartoonists of the
day, Courbet also produced many far more accessible works
that appealed to collectors and yet remained honest expressions of his robust style. Count Nieuwerkerke, Director of
the Beaux-Arts in the Second Empire, purchased with funds
from the Emperor's civil list a landscape called *Le ruisseau
couvert* (*The Shaded Stream*), painted in 1865, which then
passed to the national collections. *La vague* (*The Wave*) was
acquired for the Musée du Luxembourg shortly after the
painter's death. *La falaise d'Etretat après l'orage* (*The Cliff at
Etretat after the Storm*), of the Salon of 1870, is a fine example
of Courbet's qualities as a landscape artist; like *The Wave*, it
was painted in 1869, while Courbet was staying at Etretat, a
small town on the Normandy coast which had been a
favourite spot for painters since the early years of the century.

76 *G. Courbet*. L'atelier du peintre. Allégorie réelle déterminant une phase de sept années de ma vie artistique (The Studio of the Painter. A Real Allegory Defining a Seven-year Phase in my Artistic Life) *359 × 598 (141.3 × 235.4). Shown at Pavillon du Réalisme, place de l'Alma, Paris 1855. Acquired 1920 with the aid of a public subscription and of the Société des Amis du Louvre*

Peasant Realism

77 *J. Breton:* Le rappel des
glaneuses (Artois) (Calling
the Gleaners Home, in the
Artois Region)
*90 × 176 (35.4 × 69.3). Salon of
1859. Gift of Napoleon III,
1862*

Jules Breton (1827–1906), educated in Antwerp and Paris,
experimented from 1849–50 onwards with large-scale Realist compositions in the style of Courbet or Alexandre
Antigna. He later concentrated on studies of agricultural
workers in the fields around his native village of Courrières,
in Artois (near Calais). His paintings of peasants are more
anecdotal than those by Millet, and he won popular acclaim
in the Second Empire for such pictures as *Le rappel des
glaneuses* (*Calling the Gleaners Home*). Regarded practically
as the official painter of peasant life, he was elected a member
of the Institut de France in 1886, at a time when Naturalism
was no longer controversial.

The mid-century pioneers of this agricultural genre were
Constant Troyon (1810–65) and Rosa Bonheur (1822–99);
Bonheur's *Labourage nivernais, le sombrage* (*Ploughing in
the Nivernais Region*), commissioned by the state in 1848, has
for succeeding generations evoked the world of George
Sand's novels.

Ernest Hébert (1817–1908) is in a slightly different
category. After winning the Prix de Rome in 1839 he made
several trips to Italy, and there abandoned history painting to
concentrate instead on scenes of popular life, following the
example set by Léopold Robert and Victor Schnetz; his
masterpiece, *La Mal'aria* (*Malaria*), in the Salon of 1850–51,
reflected the prevailing Realist vein. His later compositions,
however, are tinged with the sentimentality that brought
him numerous commissions and great success as a painter of
female portraits.

78

78 C. Troyon: Garde-chasse
arrêté près de ses chiens
(Gamekeeper Standing with
his Dogs), 1854
117 × 90 (46.1 × 35.4). Bequest
of Alfred Chauchard, 1909

79 R. Bonheur: Labourage
nivernais (Ploughing in the
Nivernais Region)
134 × 260 (52.8 × 102.4).
Commissioned 1848. Salon of
1849

80 E. Hébert: La Mal'aria
(Malaria), 1848–49
135 × 193 (53.1 × 76). Salon of
1850–51. Acquired 1851

79

80

71

81

81 *G. Guillaumet:* Le Sahara,
ou Le désert (The Sahara, or
The Desert), *1867*
*110 × 200 (43.3 × 78.7). Salon
of 1868. Gift of the artist's
family, 1888*

82 *E. Fromentin:* Chasse au
faucon en Algérie; la curée
(Falconry in Algeria;
Distributing the Quarry)
*162.5 × 118 (64 × 46.5). Salon
of 1863. Acquired 1863*

82

Orientalism

The Orient, as seen from nineteenth-century France, consisted of the Muslim countries of the Mediterranean, either as they existed in the imagination – for example in Ingres' *Odalisques* – or as they were actually experienced at first hand: the Holy Land and Eastern Turkey, painted by Charles Tournemine (1812–72); Egypt, in the works of Léon Belly (1827–77), among them the impressive *Pélerins allant à la Mecque* (*Pilgrims Travelling to Mecca*) of the Salon of 1861; and above all North Africa, which Delacroix had described after a visit in 1832 as a place where the ancient civilizations lived on. Apart from the obvious attraction of new subject matter, with its glimpses of a lost Eden, there was also the dazzling quality of the light, which spurred the painters to transform their palettes. The Romanticism of Delacroix, Decamps, Chassériau and, later in the day, Henri Regnault, gave way during the Second Empire to an increasing Naturalism, a trend noted in 1861 by the brothers Jules and Edmond de Goncourt in their novel *Manette Salomon*.

Eugène Fromentin (1820–76) visited Algeria on several occasions between 1846 and 1853, and in 1857 and 1859 published two accounts of his travels, *Un été dans le Sahara* and *Une année dans le Sahel*. These trips were to furnish him with subject matter for the rest of his life, and, drawing on his memories, he painted numerous imaginary scenes and picturesque reconstructions such as *Chasse au faucon en Algérie: la curée* (*Falconry in Algeria: Distributing the Quarry*) acquired for the Musée du Luxembourg at the Salon of 1863, a brilliantly coloured canvas with drawing of an almost Ingres-like perfection.

More obviously in the Naturalist spirit is the painting of Gustave Guillaumet (1840–87), who renounced the traditional study period in Rome and went instead to North Africa, making some ten trips in all.

Photographers, too, played their part in the discovery of the Orient. One of the first to visit Egypt was Maxime Du Camp, who went there in 1849 with his friend Gustave Flaubert and afterwards wrote about his experiences in a book with photographic illustrations, reproduced in association with the printer Blanquart-Evrard. Published in 1852, it was the first publication of its type and became the model for a whole generation of photographers well represented in the Musée d'Orsay, including J. B. Greene, F. Teynard, T. Devéria and A. Salzmann.

83 *Carolus-Duran:* La dame
au gant (Lady with a Glove),
1869
228 × 164 (89.8 × 64.6).
Madame Carolus-Duran, née
*Pauline Croizette
(1839–1912), painter. Salon of
1869. Acquired 1875*

84 *J. J. Tissot:* Portrait de
Mademoiselle L. L., ou Jeune
femme en veste rouge
(Young Woman in a Red
Jacket), *1864*
*124 × 99 (48.8 × 39). Salon of
1864. Acquired 1907*

85 *A. Stevens:* Ce qu'on
appelle le vagabondage, ou
Les chasseurs de Vincennes
(What People Call Vagrancy,
or The Hunters of
Vincennes), *c. 1854*
*132 × 162 (52 × 63.8). World
Fair, Paris, 1855. Bequest of
the painter Léon Lhermitte,
1925*

83

84

85

Further aspects of Realism; Fantin-Latour

Other painters allied themselves with Realism in their choice of modern themes, but retained a meticulous traditional technique. This official Realism, always in the best of taste, is represented by Alfred Stevens (1823–1906), James Tissot (1836–1902) and Carolus-Duran (1838–1910). The modernity of these fashionable painters consisted in an idealized image of an elegant and charming bourgeoisie.

Stevens studied in Brussels under a pupil of Jacques-Louis David and then moved to Paris, where he made his Salon début with paintings on humanitarian themes, such as *Ce qu'on appelle le vagabondage* (*What Is Called Vagrancy*). The picture is a powerful, frieze-like composition with flattened perspective and simplified forms, but the mood is one of melodramatic pathos. A friend of Manet, Stevens did on occasion paint Naturalist scenes such as *La baignoire* (*The Bath*), also in the Musée d'Orsay, but his fame depended on his evocations of the affluent bourgeois world.

Attention to detail in the setting, and meticulous rendering of costumes, characterize the work of Tissot, who started out as a painter of historical genre scenes, represented in the Musée d'Orsay by his sparkling *Faust et Marguerite* (*Faust and Gretchen*). Patronized by the rich and famous, Tissot

86 *T. Ribot:* Saint Sébastien, martyr (St Sebastian) *97 × 130 (38.2 × 51.2). Salon of 1865. Acquired 1865*

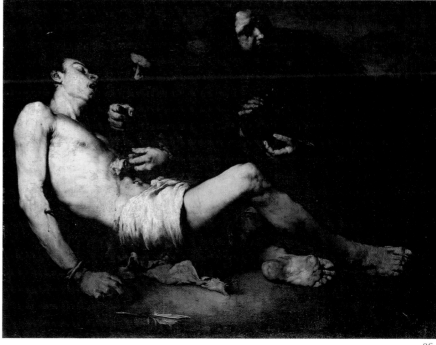

75

87 *H. Fantin-Latour:* Un
coin de table (Corner of a
Table), *1872*
*160 × 225 (63 × 88.6). Left to
right: P. Verlaine,
A. Rimbaud, E. Bonnier,
L. Valade, E. Blémont,
J. Aicard, E. D'Hervilly,
C. Pelletan. Salon of 1872. Gift
of Monsieur and Madame
Léon-Emile Petitdidier,
known as Blémont, but
retained by them for their
lifetimes, 1911; retention
abandoned, 1920*

88 *H. Fantin-Latour:* Un
atelier aux Batignolles (A
Studio in the Batignolles
Quarter), *1870*
*204 × 273.5 (80.3 × 107.7). Left
to right: O. Schölderer,
E. Manet, P. A. Renoir,
Z. Astruc, E. Zola, E. Maître,
F. Bazille, C. Monet. Salon of
1870. Acquired 1892*

breathed new life into the traditionally static form of the society portrait, a fine example being his portrait of an unknown *Young Woman,* identified as *L.L.* (1864).

La dame au gant (*Lady with a Glove*) is typical of Carolus-Duran's portraiture; the dark colours and the spirited handling reflect the artist's admiration for Spanish painting. The anecdotal detail of the dropped glove is a reminder that the society portrait is really a genre scene, and that bourgeois Realism is an undemanding option.

Théodule Ribot (1823–91) received a traditional training as a pupil of Auguste Glaize. He specialized mostly in domestic interiors, often introducing everyday objects and members of his family as in *La ravaudeuse* (*Woman Darning*), in the Musée d'Orsay. His *Saint Sébastien* (*St Sebastian*) was acquired for the nation at the Salon of 1865. His predilection for religious subjects sets him apart from the other Realists, although it indicates not so much intensity of feeling as admiration for seventeenth-century Spanish art, and for José Ribera in particular.

Henri Fantin-Latour (1836–1904) studied under Horace Lecoq de Boisbaudran, learning from him the importance of visual memory in drawing. He formed his artistic allegiances as the result of copying paintings in the Louvre, and his first major composition was *Hommage à Delacroix* (*Homage to Delacroix*), inspired by the Dutch group-portraits of the seventeenth century. Fantin-Latour was a friend of Manet and the future Impressionists, who appear in *Un atelier aux Batignolles* (*A Studio in the Batignolles Quarter*), of 1870. He shared with them a taste for modern life and a dislike of anecdotal painting. His *Un Coin de table* (*Corner of a Table*) of 1872, takes liberties with conventional perspective in order to make the figures of Verlaine and Rimbaud the central feature of the composition. This is the only known portrait of the latter.

In the latter half of his career Fantin-Latour painted numerous still-lifes, which show meticulous observation and an interest in light effects. His rather austere portraits focus all the attention on the face, the simplicity of the presentation emphasizing the character of the sitter. But the paintings in which he took the greatest pleasure were poetic compositions, transpositions into visual terms of his response to literature or to the music of Wagner, Berlioz or Schumann.

87

88

Whistler

James Abbott McNeill Whistler (1834–1903) was barely more than twenty when he left the United States and went to study painting in France. Thenceforth he was to divide his life between Paris and London. A friend of Courbet and of Fantin-Latour – who painted him alongside Baudelaire, Manet and others in his *Homage to Delacroix* – Whistler was from the outset inclined towards Realism, and his work therefore received a frosty reception in official circles. He was, too, a fervent admirer of Far Eastern art, and in particular Japanese prints, whose introduction to the West had such a profound influence on so many European artists.

This love of decorative simplicity was reflected in the extreme delicacy of his palette, founded in exquisite harmonies of finely graduated, understated colour. Famous for his views of the Thames, painted in a quivering haze reminiscent of some of the effects achieved by Monet at a certain period, Whistler was also a successful portraitist. His *Arrangement en gris et noir, portrait de la mère de l'artiste* (*Arrangement in Grey and Black, Portrait of the Artist's Mother*), of 1871, entered the French national collections in 1891 thanks to the efforts of his friend the poet Stéphane Mallarmé and of the critic Théodore Duret, who knew Manet and the Impressionists and admired Whistler's work. This rather austere painting has become the artist's best-known work.

Aspects of
provincial painting

90 *A. Monticelli:* Nature
morte au pichet blanc (Still-
life with White Jug)
*49 × 63 (19.3 × 24.8). Acquired
1937*

91 *P. Guigou:* Lavandière
(Washerwoman), *1860
81 × 59 (31.9 × 23.2). Gift of
Paul Rosenberg, 1912*

In the second half of the nineteenth century Paris was the
centre of artistic life in France. Nevertheless, there were
certain figures of powerful originality, a little apart from the
mainstream, who lived and worked in relative isolation in the
provinces. They in turn attracted admirers and imitators, and
so founded regional schools of painting. The most obvious
example is F. A. Ravier (1814–95), who, although initially a
pupil of Corot, belongs to the School of Lyon. His free
handling of skyscapes reflects the influence of Turner.
Another outsider was Adolphe Monticelli (1824–86), who
studied in Marseille and continued to work in the South of
France even after he became nominally resident in Paris. His
admiration for Delacroix and for the virtuosity of Diaz led
him to develop a brilliant technique using heavy impasto,
which came as a revelation to the young Vincent van
Gogh. Also a southerner, Monticelli's friend Paul Guigou
(1833–71) was a great admirer of Courbet. He was chiefly
interested in the effects produced by the strong sunlight of
Provence, and his studies on that theme are somewhat
reminiscent of those by his young contemporary Frédéric
Bazille.

90

91

Plein-air landscape painting

In the first half of the nineteenth century there were numerous landscape painters who insisted on the need to observe nature faithfully and to set down at speed, working in the open air (*en plein-air*) and with the motif before them, the ephemeral character of the scene that presented itself to their eyes. In England there were, most notably, John Constable, J. M. W. Turner and Richard Bonington, and in France a line from Paul-Henri de Valenciennes through to Corot and the Barbizon School. Their heirs, in the middle years of the century, were J. B. Jongkind and Eugène Boudin, who developed these principles in the 1850s, each in his own distinctive manner. Jongkind (1819–91) was Dutch but lived and worked in France. He evolved a very free and spirited technique, which, combined with his Realist inclinations, was enough to ensure his presence – alongside Manet – at the Salon des Refusés of 1863; the picture by which he was represented was a landscape, *Ruines du château de Rosemont* (*The Ruined Château at Rosemont*). He was a watercolourist of exceptional talent and produced many striking landscapes of Holland, the Ile-de-France, Paris and Montmartre, the

92 *E. Boudin:* La plage de Trouville (The Beach at Trouville), *1864*
26 × 48 (10.2 × 18.9). Gift of Dr Eduardo Mollard, 1961

93

Normandy coast and the Isère. The French national
museums are fortunate to have in their possession a superb
series of his watercolours, thanks to the generosity of the
collector Etienne Moreau-Nélaton.

Eugène Boudin (1824–98) studied for a brief period in
Paris and was advised by Isabey and Troyon. Corot and
Courbet were the painters whose example he admired, but it
was above all his friend Jongkind who influenced him in the
course he would follow. Boudin was born in Honfleur and
died in Deauville: his painting is rooted in that area of the
Normandy coast where he spent so much of his life. Later,
when he was famous and could afford to travel, he painted
also in Brittany, around Bordeaux, in the South of France,
Venice and Holland. It was in 1862 that he began to paint
scenes showing the crowds of elegant summer visitors on the
beaches of Deauville and Trouville – a theme that verged
almost on genre painting. Yet the apparent superficiality of
the subject seemed to release his powers of expression. These
bright paintings, pulsating with light, were to make a deep
impression on the young Claude Monet, whose family lived
in Le Havre. 'If I have become a painter, I owe it to Eugène
Boudin,' he wrote, underlining the importance of the role
Boudin played in the genesis of Impressionism. Monet also
knew Jongkind well, and stayed with Bazille at the Ferme
Saint-Siméon near Honfleur. This simple farmhouse became
famous for the numbers of artists who stayed there in the
nineteenth century, among them Diaz, Troyon, Daubigny,
Corot and Courbet. There are major works by these painters,
sometimes called the Pre-Impressionists, in the Eduardo
Mollard collection, which, in accordance with the
benefactor's wishes, is kept together in the Musée d'Orsay.

Manet

When Edouard Manet (1832–83), a friend of the notorious poet Baudelaire, sent in to the 1863 Salon jury his *Déjeuner sur l'herbe*, then known as *Le bain* (*Bathing*), he was already, in the eyes of the younger artists and critics, a leader of what we would now term the avant-garde (although he had received official approval in 1861 for a daringly free exercise in the 'Spanish vein'). *Le bain* was rejected; and indeed the jury turned down so many paintings that year that Napoleon III himself opened a supplementary Salon. This was the famous Salon des Refusés, and there *Le bain* was an overnight sensation.

The picture was regarded as shocking both because it was painted with the freedom of a sketch and because of its subject – never mind that it was derived from an engraving by Raphael, the very painter most revered by the Ecole des

94 *E. Manet:* Le déjeuner sur l'herbe (Luncheon on the Grass), *1863*
208 × 264.5 (81.9 × 104.1).
Salon des Refusés, 1863. Gift of Etienne Moreau-Nélaton, 1906

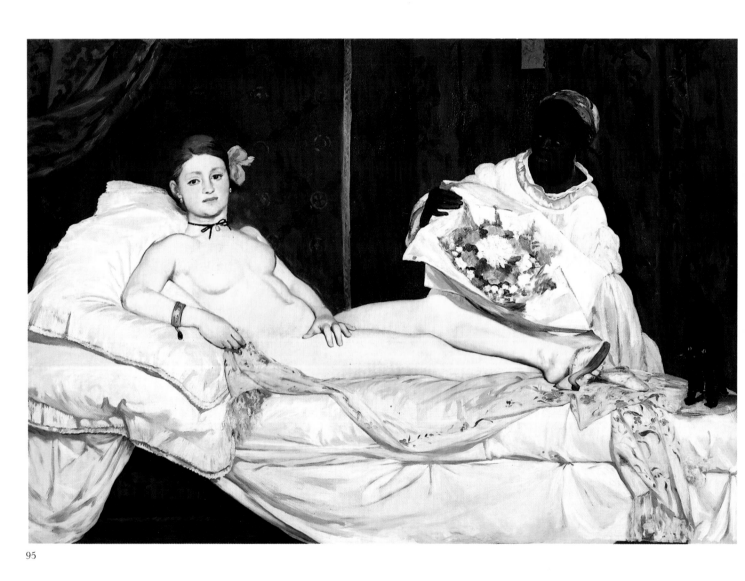

95

95 *E. Manet:* Olympia, *1863*
130.5 × 190 (51.4 × 74.8). Salon
of 1865. Presented to the
nation as the result of a public
subscription raised by Claude
Monet, 1890

Beaux-Arts. Certainly the subject was provocative: a naked woman posing unconcernedly in the company of two well-dressed young men who looked like students. 'Monsieur Manet seeks to make his name by shocking the bourgeoisie ... his taste is corrupted by a love of the bizarre,' wrote a critic of the day, failing to understand what Manet was trying to do – which was to transpose into a modern setting a traditional theme of Renaissance Italy, to create a contemporary version of the 'pastoral interlude' or *concert champêtre.*

An even greater scandal was sparked off by *Olympia* (1863) at the Salon of 1865. Once again Manet had transformed an idealized nude – Titian's *Venus of Urbino* – into a provocative and quasi-photographic image that showed a hidden side of life in the Second Empire: a naked prostitute with a challenging gaze, lying on her bed. Today we can still respond to the provoking fascination of this nude, but the 'immorality' of the context has lost its force. The painting is above all an extraordinary *tour de force*, both for its technique and its subject matter, a masterpiece of sensual expression that links the great classical art of the past with modern painting. The female figure who in her own day was seen as a 'redhead of out-and-out ugliness', a 'yellow-bellied odalisque', a 'Queen of Spades', looks now – because of the handling and the dazzling use of colour, the contradictions and the humour, even because of that brazen stare – like a Mona Lisa of the modern age.

As a young man Emile Zola was an astute and far-sighted critic. Manet painted his portrait as a gesture of gratitude for the impassioned defence of his work issued by the twenty-eight-year-old writer. In this portrait Zola is surrounded by

96

97

objects reflecting his tastes and concerns: Japanese prints, engravings by Manet, Naturalist novels and, lying under his pen, the little blue book in which he wrote his defence of Manet.

At the next Salon, of 1869, Manet exhibited *Le balcon* (*The Balcony*), a contemporary treatment of a theme used by Goya. Seated in the foreground, in front of the painter Antoine Guillemet and the young violinist Fanny Claus, is one of Manet's favourite models, the beautiful Berthe Morisot, soon to join the Impressionist ranks as a painter in her own right.

Spurned by the authorities in the painter's lifetime, Manet's work came to be represented in the state museums only as the result of generous donations by private individuals and friends. In 1890 Claude Monet organized a campaign to purchase *Olympia* for the nation from Manet's widow. *The Balcony* entered the national collections as part of the controversial Gustave Caillebotte bequest, followed by *Le déjeuner sur l'herbe* in the Etienne Moreau-Nélaton gift of 1906, and *Le fifre* (*The Fifer*) in the collection of Count Isaac de Camondo, left to the state in 1911. These and other gifts and acquisitions have ensured that the museum now possesses an outstanding selection of Manet's works, including some of his finest pastels.

The Impressionists before 1870

In the early 1860s the private studio class run by Charles Gleyre, a painter of Swiss origin, became the focus of activity for a number of young painters. Auguste Renoir enrolled in 1861, to be joined shortly afterwards by Frédéric Bazille, newly arrived from Montpellier, and later Claude Monet and Alfred Sisley. These painters formed a group united by common ideals, in particular a hostility towards academic art and an inclination towards Realism. Renoir (1841–1919), with no family money behind him, managed to keep his head above water by painting portraits, among them one of his friend Sisley's father, accepted for the Salon of 1865. Renoir was from the outset attracted to the human figure, whether the model was his companion Lise Tréhot – who must have posed for the small *Femme demi-nue couchée* (*Reclining Nude*) in the Musée d'Orsay – or his friend Bazille, who gave him shelter on more than one occasion during these difficult years. He admired Courbet and Delacroix, but he was also influenced by Manet and Monet. Bazille (1841–70), who died young in the battle in the Franco-Prussian War, was another figure painter. *Réunion de famille* (*Family Gathering*), one of his most accomplished pictures, was executed in 1867 and exhibited at the Salon of 1868. It shows members of his family posing on the terrace of a house near Montpellier. A strong debt to Manet is apparent in the brilliance of the colouring, the bold presentation of human forms and the intensity of the light exaggerating the contrasts, but there is also an affinity with Monet, whom Bazille frequently accompanied on painting expeditions. Of all the group, Monet (1840–1926) was regarded as the most 'advanced'. As a young man in Le Havre he was decisively influenced by Boudin and Jongkind, who encouraged him to paint out of doors, and his early landscapes – which also owe much to Daubigny – have a freshness and confidence that did not escape the notice of the critics. Responding to Manet's picture of the same title, Monet painted his own large-scale composition *Le déjeuner sur l'herbe* (1865), two sections of which survive in the Musée d'Orsay, and then *Femmes au jardin* (*Women in the Garden*), rejected by the Salon of 1867, which includes a portrait of his future wife, Camille. This large and ambitious composition was started *in situ* as a *plein-*

98

99

100

air painting (which, given the size of the canvas, was in itself a major achievement), the purpose being to retain the freshness of the original vision in the finished work; the canvas was in fact extensively reworked in the studio. The sharp silhouetting of the figures, the contrasts of light and shade, and the choice of a subject from modern life with no anecdotal detail whatsoever, could not but offend the conservative Salon jury, who maintained an implacable hostility towards this style of painting which had grown up in the wake of Courbet and Manet. It fell to Zola to defend Monet's picture, just as he had pleaded the cause of Manet and Pissarro before him. That Monet was undeterred by the virulence of the attacks is brilliantly attested by the other masterpieces of this period in the Musée d'Orsay, notably *La pie* (*The Magpie*) and *Hôtel des Roches-Noires à Trouville* (*Hôtel des Roches-Noires, Trouville*).

100 *C. Monet:* La pie (The Magpie), c. *1868–69*
89 × 130 (35 × 51.2). Acquired 1984

101 *F. Bazille:* Réunion de famille (The Artist's family on a Terrace), *1867*
152 × 230 (59.8 × 90.6). Salon of 1868. Acquired in association with Marc Bazille, the artist's brother, 1905

101

Drawing and watercolour

102 *J. B. Jongkind:*
Autoportrait sous le soleil
(Self-portrait, sunshine),
c. *1850–60*
*Watercolour. 20 × 17
(7.9 × 6.7). Gift of Etienne
Moreau-Nélaton, 1906*

103 *G. Doré:* Catastrophe du
Mont-Cervin; la chute
(Tragedy on the Matterhorn;
the Fall), *1865*
*Pen and brown ink, India ink
wash, brown wash, highlights
in white gouache. 79 × 58.5
(31 × 23). Gift of
Mademoiselle de Viefville,
1952*

Complementing the collections of painting, sculpture and decorative arts in the Musée d'Orsay, there will also be opportunities to see drawings by the various artists represented. These temporary exhibitions (it being possible to display the drawings only for restricted periods and in precise lighting conditions) are intended to serve very much as an introduction to the permanent collections of the Cabinet des Dessins in the Louvre. That vast repository includes examples of work, both individual items and major series, by most of the leading artists of the period covered by the Musée d'Orsay. A mention of just a few of the artists represented from the early years of that period will suggest something of the richness and diversity of the collections: the fantastical and meticulous storytelling of Gustave Doré is worlds away from the pungent Realism of Daumier or the poetic Realism of Millet (particularly well represented here) or from Jongkind, who anticipated the Impressionist style in a series of watercolours donated to the Louvre as part of the Moreau-Nélaton collection.

102   103

104

105

104 *J. F. Millet:* Le bouquet
de marguerites (The Bunch
of Daisies), *1871–74*
Pastel. 68 × 83 (26.8 × 32.7).
*Acquired out of income from
bequest of Madame Dol-Lair,
1949*

105 *H. Daumier:* Le
défenseur (Counsel for the
Defence)
*Pen and black ink,
watercolour and gouache over
a pencil outline. 19 × 29
(7.5 × 11.4). Acquired in lieu
of estate duties, 1977*

Photography

106

106 *F. Nadar:* Portrait d'une
antillaise (Portrait of a West
Indian Woman), c. *1855*
Salt print from wet-collodion
glass-plate negative. 25 × 19
(9.8 × 7.5). Acquired 1981

107 *G. Le Gray:* Le vapeur
(The Steamer), *1857*
Albumen print from two wet-
collodion glass plate negatives.
32 × 41.3 (12.6 × 16.3).
Acquired 1985

Long overlooked and even now largely neglected, the
photography of the nineteenth century is given proper
coverage for the first time with the opening of the Musée
d'Orsay. The displays have been organized to illustrate the
significant developments in the history of photography, both
in France and abroad, starting with the daguerreotype and
ending with the snapshot and the rise of the 'pictorialist'
movement. At this point the Musée National d'Art Moderne
in the Centre Pompidou takes over, with the abstract and
experimental photography that first appeared in Europe and
America towards the end of the First World War.

When work was started on assembling the Musée d'Orsay
collection, in 1979, it was decided to concentrate specifically
on photography as a creative art, thus supplying a different
emphasis from the archive of the Bibliothèque Nationale,
which, according to a law passed in 1851, receives copies of all
commercially used photographs. The principal criterion of
'artistic' quality is originality in the interpretation of subject
matter, and yet some of the most imaginative uses of the
medium in the nineteenth century were in the form of
documentary records – one thinks in particular of the views
of Egypt by J. B. Greene (1832–57) or the Parisian scenes of
Eugène Atget (1857–1923). The museum is not interested
exclusively in the work of professional photographers; it is
also concerned with artists working in other fields who at
certain times experimented with photography for particular
purposes of their own, whether visual artists (Degas, Bonnard, Gallé) or writers (such as Victor Hugo or Lewis
Carroll).

The Musée d'Orsay collections are particularly well
endowed with the works of the so-called 'primitives', active
first in England and later in France when photographs first
began to be printed on paper (*c.* 1850–60). Within that short
period the expressive potential of the new medium was
explored with startling inventiveness and variety, already
suggesting many of the techniques that were to be developed
in the future.

111

112

113

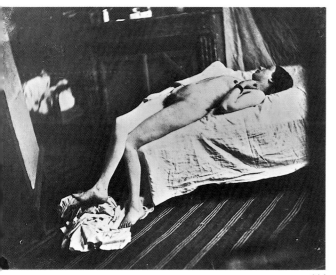

114

115

Architecture
and town-planning

116

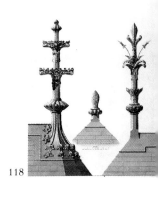

117

118

116 *V. Ruprich-Robert:*
Floral ornament: ash bud,
1866–69
Crayon and pencil. 41.5 × 33.8
(16.3 × 13.3). Gift of Ruprich-
Robert family, 1981

117 *V. Ruprich-Robert:*
Floral ornament: thistle,
c. *1866–69*
Crayon and pencil. 41.5 × 33.8
(16.3 × 13.3). Gift of Ruprich-
Robert family, 1981

118 *Firme Monduit:* Designs
for finials, *late 19th century*
Pen and black ink, grey wash,
white highlights. 74.8 × 51.2
(29.4 × 20.2). Gift of Madame
G. Pasquier-Monduit, 1983

119 *A. Gosset:* Sainte-
Clotilde, Rheims, Elevations
and Section, *1898–1900*
Crayon, pen and black and red
ink, grey wash, watercolour,
highlights in white gouache.
66 × 160 (26 × 63). Acquired
1985

In architecture, the second half of the nineteenth century was a time of expansion. There was extensive urban redevelopment, not only in Haussmann's Paris but in comparable programmes in provincial France and abroad. A vast construction programme was undertaken – railway stations, factories, town halls, museums, schools and colleges, grand hotels. Technology was making rapid strides; iron was in widespread use, and concrete began to make an appearance. The architecture of this period can all too easily seem to be bogged down in a more or less slavish imitation of bygone styles. Yet the historicism of Eugène Viollet-le-Duc (1814–79) or Victor Ruprich-Robert (1859–1953) cannot simply be dismissed as a sterile reproduction of the forms of a previous age; these architects were, in their own way, as interested as was the Arts and Crafts Movement in England in extending their designs to include even the smallest detail of interior decoration. Using medieval architecture as a source of new design ideas, they paved the way for the movement we now call Art Nouveau. Among the more prominent landmarks of the architecture of this period are buildings erected for the World Fairs held in Paris between 1855 and 1900, notably the Palais de l'Industrie (1855) and the Eiffel Tower (1889).

119

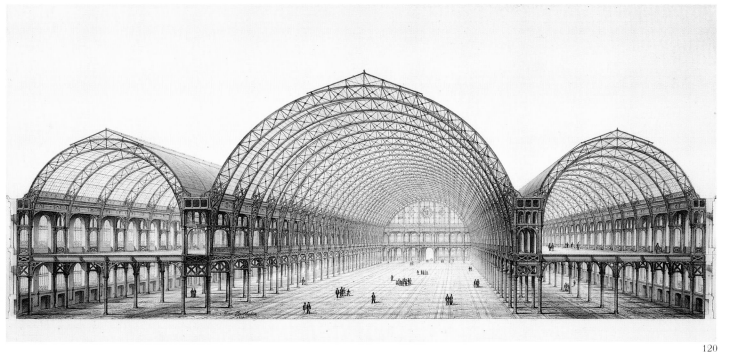

120

121

122

120 *M. Berthelin:* Palais de l'Industrie: cross section, *1854 Pen and black ink, watercolour. 31 × 67.3 (12.2 × 26.5). Acquired 1979*

121 *L. E. Lheureux:* Design for a monument celebrating the French Revolution *Perspective drawing. Crayon, pen and ink, wash, watercolour, gold highlights. 48 × 86.5 (18.9 × 34.1). Salon des Artistes français, 1889. Acquired 1981*

122 *A. Bourgade:* Calligram or word-picture of the Eiffel Tower, *1889 Drawing. 80 × 57 (31.5 × 22.4). Eiffel archives. Gift of Mademoiselle Solange Granet, Madame Bernard Granet and children, descendants of Gustave Eiffel, 1981*

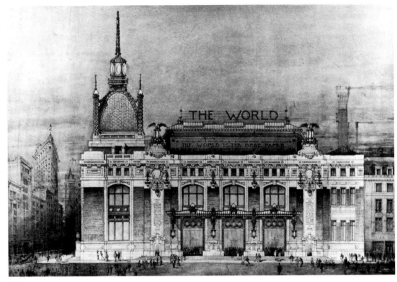

123

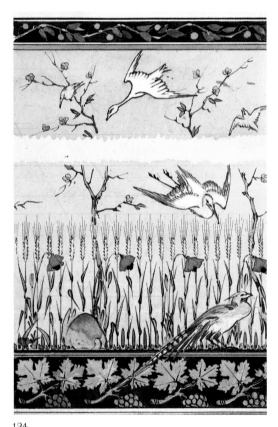

124

123 *M. Boille:* Student
project: newspaper offices
Crayon and watercolour.
54.2 × 81.8 (21.3 × 32.2). Gift
of Pierre and Jacques Boille,
sons of the architect, 1982

124 *E. Viollet-le-Duc:*
Furnishing fabric, design for
'Histoire d'une maison',
c. *1870–73*
Watercolour. 19.6 × 11.2
(7.7 × 4.4). Acquired 1980

125 *G. M. Niedecken:* Design
for the living-room of the
M.E.P. Irving house, Decatur,
Ill.
The house was built by Frank
Lloyd Wright in 1909–10. Pen
and black ink and watercolour
on canvas. 71 × 66 (28 × 26).
Acquired 1985

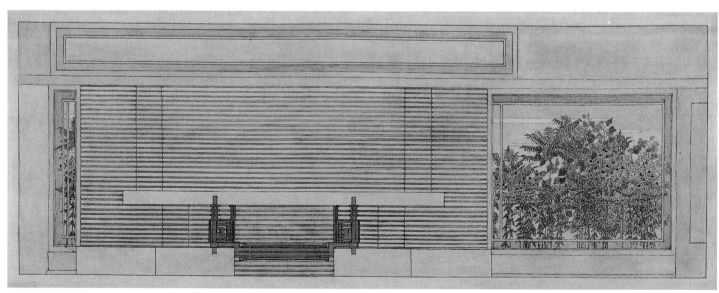

125

Impressionism

Tired of constant rebuffs from the Salon jury, a few artists decided in the spring of 1874 to stage an independent exhibition of their works in rooms on the Boulevard des Capucines in Paris. Among them were Edgar Degas, Auguste Renoir, Camille Pissarro, Paul Cézanne, Alfred Sisley, Armand Guillaumin, Berthe Morisot, and Claude Monet, who showed a canvas called *Impression, soleil levant* (*Impression: Sunrise*). An incensed critic coined the mocking epithet 'impressionist', and the name stuck. There was one notable absentee from their ranks, a painter who had crossed swords more than once with the Salon jury and chose not to risk further offence. This was Edouard Manet, who, by public

126 *C. Monet:* Régates à Argenteuil (Sailing Boats at Argenteuil), c. *1872* *48 × 75 (18.9 × 29.5). Bequest of Gustave Caillebotte, 1894*

126

127

127 *P. A. Renoir:* Etude: torse, effet de soleil (Study: Nude in the Sunlight), *1875 81 × 65 (31.9 × 25.6). Shown at second Impressionist exhibition, 1876. Bequest of Gustave Caillebotte, 1894*

128 *P. A. Renoir:* Bal du Moulin de la Galette (Dancing at the Moulin de la Galette), *1876 131 × 175 (51.6 × 68.9). Exhibited at the third Impressionist exhibition, 1877. Bequest of Gustave Caillebotte, 1894*

and critics alike, was regarded as the leader of the group, which assembled regularly at the Café Guerbois and later the Café de la Nouvelle Athènes. The experiment of a group exhibition was repeated in 1876, 1877, 1879, 1880, 1881, 1882 and 1886. Although there was some internal dissension and a number of defections, there were always newcomers keen to participate, among them Gustave Caillebotte (1848–94), in 1876, who helped his friends by buying their paintings. He left his magnificent collection to the nation in 1894, and so ensured, in the face of fierce opposition at the time, the presence in the state collections of a superb body of Impressionist painting, today one of the glories of the Musée d'Orsay. In 1879, at the time of the fourth independent exhibition, the group was joined by Mary Cassatt, a friend of Degas, and also by Albert Lebourg and Paul Gauguin, closely associated with Pissarro. The participation of Georges Seurat and Paul Signac in the last exhibition, of 1886, effectively marked the end of one era and the beginning of the next.

It was only because of the loyalty of a small number of collectors and critics, among them Paul Durand-Ruel, that these painters managed to survive the hardships of those difficult years. Most of them had started their careers in the 1860s and had reached artistic maturity without receiving official recognition. By then, though they were still united in their opposition to academic art and in their desire to be painters of the modern age, their divergent personalities had begun to lead them in very different directions.

Degas

Edgar Degas (1834–1917) figured prominently in the first exhibition of the embryonic Impressionist group in 1874. Although his career in the 1860s had appeared to be proceeding along traditional lines, it was above all his choice of subjects from contemporary reality – the ballet, Parisian cafés, working girls, milliners and washerwomen, the races – and the Naturalism of his portraits that transformed him within the space of a few years into one of the most masterly exponents of the 'new painting'. Degas' love of unusual angles and viewpoints was accompanied by precise draughtsmanship and bold, flowing forms; his palette, which was initially dark and austere, later expanded to include a range of acid tones.

139 *E. Degas:* Au café, *dit* L'absinthe (At the Café, *known as* Absinthe), *1876 92 × 68 (36.2 × 26.8). Bequest of Isaac de Camondo, 1911*

140 *E. Degas:* Chevaux de courses devant les tribunes (Race-horses in Front of the Stands), *c. 1869 46 × 61 (18.1 × 24). Bequest of Isaac de Camondo, 1911*

139

140

141 *E. Degas:* L'étoile (The Star), c. *1878*
Pastel. 60 × 44 (23.6 × 17.3).
Bequest of Gustave Caillebotte, 1894

142 *E. Degas:* Les repasseuses (Women Ironing), c. *1884*
76 × 81.5 (29.9 × 32.1). Bequest of Isaac de Camondo, 1911

143 *E. Degas:* Grande danseuse habillée (Little Dancer of Fourteen Years or Large Dancer, Clothed)
Bronze cast of the original wax model shown at sixth Impressionist exhibition, 1881. 98 (38.6). Acquired 1930 through the generosity of the artist's heirs and the metal founder, Hébrard.

141

142

Manet

144 *E. Manet:* Sur la plage
(On the Beach), *1873*
*59.5 × 73 (23.4 × 28.7). Gift of
Jean Edouard Dubrujeaud,
subject to a life interest, 1953;
entered national collection
1970*

145 *E. Manet:* Georges
Clemenceau *(1841–1929),
1879*
*94.5 × 74 (37.2 × 29.1). Gift of
Mrs Louisine W. Havemeyer,
1927*

Sur la plage (*On the Beach*) was painted in 1873 at Berck-sur-Mer, presumably as a *plein-air* picture. It represents Manet's wife Suzanne, who frequently modelled for her husband, and his brother Eugène, shortly to marry Berthe Morisot. A work like this illustrates just how different Manet's style of painting was from that of his young Impressionist friends, even where the subject matter was analogous. Manet's vision was essentially a blend of classical and Japanese influences: the gradation of shades of grey in the foreground is worthy of Frans Hals or Velázquez. Around 1874 he painted extensively in Argenteuil, with Monet, but refused to take part in the group exhibitions of the so-called independents, continuing to submit his work to the official Salon in spite of the unrelenting hostility of the critics. Afflicted with partial paralysis in 1880, he died in 1883.

The Musée d'Orsay is the possessor of a fine portrait by Manet of Georges Clemenceau (1841–1929), a fitting tribute to the politician who did so much to help the Impressionists. It was he who gave official blessing to Monet's campaign to purchase Manet's *Olympia* for the Louvre, in 1907, and he was also responsible for the commission issued to Monet in the latter years of his life for the great sequence of paintings of waterlilies (*Nymphéas*) in the Orangerie.

144

145

Renoir, Monet, Pissarro

For all the artists in the Impressionist group, the early 1880s were a time for taking stock, if not actually one of artistic crisis. Renoir had been exhibiting again at the Salon since 1878, enjoying a fair degree of success. His improved financial situation enabled him to travel, and he visited Algeria in 1881; the Musée d'Orsay possesses several major canvases from this trip, notable for their treatment of the strong southern light and for the many echoes of Delacroix. A trip to Italy later that year led him to rediscover the Renaissance masters he had admired in the Louvre as a young man, and his first-hand experience of classical antiquity, for example the paintings of Pompeii, had an undoubted influence on his own work. A new concern for drawing is apparent in two major compositions of 1883, *Danse à la ville* (*Dance in the City*) – the female model is Suzanne Valadon, later a painter herself and the mother of Maurice Utrillo – and *Danse à la campagne* (*Dance in the Country*), where the model is Aline Charigot, later to become Renoir's wife. Renoir's palette became simpler and took on the acid tones that typify his work at this period. Yet with *Jeunes filles au piano* (*Young Girls at the Piano*), the first painting by Renoir ever purchased for the nation (at Mallarmé's suggestion, in 1892), there is clear evidence of a move towards an altogether softer style and warmer colours. Renoir continued to paint the relaxed and charming scenes he preferred, returning again and again to the theme of female *Bathers* (*Baigneuses*), which found its culmination in the great composition of 1918–19, executed in the last few months of his life. Crippled with rheumatism, the old painter had retired to Cagnes-sur-Mer in the South of France, and there he produced this dazzling pictorial testament, in which the human forms, sensual and exuberantly coloured in the manner of Rubens, blend and coalesce in an incandescent landscape.

Like Renoir, Monet was active well into the twentieth century, the different stages of his artistic development being directly linked to particular motifs, which in turn were conditioned largely by his place of residence. Late in 1878 he

146 *C. Pissarro:* Jeune fille à
la baguette (Peasant Girl
with Stick), *1881*
*81 × 65 (31.9 × 25.6). Bequest
of Isaac de·Camondo, 1911*

147 *P. A. Renoir:* Jeunes
filles au piano (Young Girls
at the Piano), *1892*
*116 × 90 (45.7 × 35.4).
Acquired 1892*

moved to Vétheuil, a small village in the Seine valley
between Paris and Rouen, and until 1891 he found his subject
matter in the surrounding area, landscapes that reflected the
changing seasons. When the Seine was frozen over during the
harsh winter of 1879–80, he produced a sequence of
paintings on this theme, several of which are in the
museum's possession. The move down river to Giverny
corresponded to a further development in his work. Monet
had always liked to produce many different interpretations of
a single motif, studying ephemeral effects of light as it altered
through the day or over the different seasons of the year. Yet
it was only with the *Meules* (*Haystacks*) that the 'series'
became a feature of his working method. He wrote to his
friend, the critic Gustave Geffroy: 'I am persisting with a
series of different effects, but at this time of the year the sun
sets so fast I cannot keep up with it ... the further I get, the
more I see that it will take a great deal of work to succeed in
conveying what I want: "instantaneity", and above all the
external "envelope", the same light spread overall.'

Other series were to follow, notably that based on Rouen
Cathedral, which although dated 1894 was in fact painted in
two bursts in 1892 and 1893; the sequence is well represented
in the Musée d'Orsay by the bequest of Comte Isaac de

148

149

Camondo, a collector with a passion for Monet's work, and by one canvas purchased by the state (coming to terms with Monet's reputation rather late in the day) in 1907.

Around the turn of the century Monet painted other series based on Giverny and London. At that time he often used canvases that were almost square, and this is also the format of his earliest paintings of waterlilies in his garden at Giverny, exhibited under the collective title *Bassin aux nymphéas* (*Waterlily Pool*). This motif was Monet's central preoccupation throughout the latter period of his career, culminating in the vast decorative scheme for the two rooms of the Musée de l'Orangerie, opened to the public in 1927 after the painter's death, but planned by him with the assistance of his devoted friend Clemenceau.

148 *P. A. Renoir:* Danse à la campagne (Dance in the Country), *1883*
180 × 90 (70.9 × 35.4).
Acquired 1979

149 *P. A. Renoir:* Danse à la ville (Dance in the City), *1883*
180 × 90 (70.9 × 35.4).
Acquired in lieu of estate duties, 1978

150   151   152

150–154 C. Monet: La cathédrale de Rouen (Rouen Cathedral)
106 × 73 (41.7 × 28.7);
100 × 65 (39.4 × 25.6);
107 × 73 (42.1 × 28.7);
107 × 73 (42.1 × 28.7); 91 × 63 (35.8 × 24.8). Although dated 1894, these five works from a series were painted in 1892 and 1893. Harmonie brune (Harmony in Brown, *153) was acquired in 1907.* Effet du matin, harmonie blanche (Morning Effect, Harmony in White, *150*), Temps gris (Overcast Weather, *151*), Plein soleil, harmonie bleue et or (Full Sunlight, Harmony in Blue and Gold, *152*), Soleil matinal, harmonie bleue (Morning Sun, Harmony in Blue, *154) were part of the bequest of Isaac de Camondo, 1911.*

Sisley's development, like Monet's, can be traced through the different motifs he adopted at various periods. After moving to Moret-sur-Loing in 1882, he worked almost exclusively on landscapes of that area. He died in 1899, too soon to experience his fame.

Pissarro was the only one of the Impressionists to take part in all the group exhibitions. His work, too, changed radically in the early 1880s. Previously a landscapist, he began to develop an interest in the human figure, embarking on a series of paintings of the peasants of Pontoise. *Jeune Fille à la baguette* (*Peasant Girl with Stick*) is a good example of his work in this period, combining sensitivity with solid construction; the alternation of fine brushwork and heavy impasto is evidence of his almost obsessive concern for technical experiment. Indeed it was this enthusiasm for new effects that led him to adopt the Neo-Impressionist or Divisionist theories of Seurat and Signac in 1886–87. It fairly rapidly became apparent that the application of strict rules did not suit his temperament, and he abandoned the method in favour of the more fluid handling that is typical of his late works – landscapes of Eragny-sur-Epte (where he moved in 1884) and views of Paris and Rouen.

Seurat and Neo-Impressionism

166

167

In the course of a brief but intensely active career Georges Seurat (1859–91) produced a small number of masterpieces, now largely dispersed in foreign museums. The result is that Seurat is relatively little known in his own country. *Une baignade, Asnières (Bathers at Asnières)*, of 1883–84, rejected by the Salon jury and exhibited at the first Salon of the Société des Artistes Indépendants in 1884, is now in London. *Une dimanche après-midi à l'Ile de la Grande Jatte (Sunday on the Island of La Grande Jatte)*, shown at the eighth and last Impressionist exhibition of 1886, is in Chicago. *Les poseuses (The Models)*, of 1886–88, is in the Barnes Foundation, Merion, Pa. The first two of these masterpieces are represented in the Musée d'Orsay by a few working sketches, the third by a number of more finished and meticulously executed studies. Otherwise, the only examples in the museum of his perfected technique, generally known as Neo-Impressionism, are one landscape, *Port-en-Bessin* (1888), and his last painting, *Le cirque (The Circus)*, of 1891. His method consisted in the application on the canvas of tiny dabs of pure, divided colour, according to a system of formal composition founded in the equilibrium of opposites, probably based on the Golden Section. In the course of a traditional classical training, Seurat had become interested in theories of line and colour, which he studied in the writings of Blanc, Rood and Chevreul, and later with his contemporary Charles Henry. Seurat hoped to found a new 'great tradition' that would build on the achievements of Impressionism, one based on his own interpretation of modernity as extending beyond subject matter to encompass rigorous 'scientific' method. In *The Circus* – not without wit – he uses the symbolism of colour and ascendant lines to convey a sense of animated movement and celebration.

Seurat's theories were taken up and developed by his friend Paul Signac (1863–1935) in a manifesto published at the end of the century, *D'Eugène Delacroix au néo-impressionnisme*. After Seurat's early death it fell to Signac to take over his mantle as leader of the movement, and he

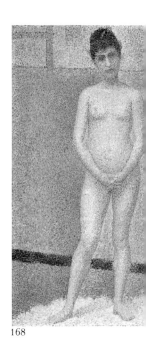

168

166–168 *G. Seurat:* Trois esquisses pour Les poseuses (Three Sketches for The Models), *1886–87*
25 × 16 (9.8 × 6.3); 24.5 × 15.5 (9.6 × 6.1); 25 × 16 (9.8 × 6.3).
Acquired 1947

169 *G. Seurat:* Le cirque (The Circus), *1891*
185.5 × 152.5 (73 × 60).
Bequest of John Quinn, 1924

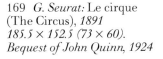

170

171

170 *G. Seurat:* Port-en-
Bessin, avant-port, marée
haute (Port-en-Bessin, Outer
Harbour, High Tide), *1888
67 × 82 (26.4 × 32.3). Proceeds
of anon. Canadian gift, 1952*

171 *P. Signac:* La bouée
rouge (The Red Buoy), *1895
81 × 65 (31.9 × 25.6). Gift of
Dr Pierre Hébert, subject to a
life interest, 1957; entered
national collection 1973*

172 *H. E. Cross:* L'air du soir
(Evening Breeze), *1894
115.5 × 163 (45.5 × 64.2). Gift
of Mme Ginette Signac, 1976*

developed a method that relied more on colour and broader brushstrokes. From the late 1890s onwards he concentrated increasingly on seascapes which, in their alliance of a true Impressionist sensibility with disciplined technique, have surprising affinities with French landscapes of the seventeenth and eighteenth centuries. Of the other members of the group, which held together until the mid 1890s (Charles Angrand, Maximilien Luce, Albert Dubois-Pillet, and for a time Camille Pissarro and Théo van Rysselberghe, among others), it was Henri-Edmond Cross (1856–1910) who, alongside Signac, remained loyal to Seurat's technique for the rest of his life. His *L'air du soir* (*Evening Breeze*), though Neo-Impressionist or 'Divisionist' in manner, demonstrates a fine aesthetic sense that is typical of the *fin de siècle* and somewhat reminiscent of the Nabis, Maurice Denis in particular.

172

Toulouse-Lautrec

Born of an aristocratic family from south-west France, Henri de Toulouse-Lautrec (1864–1901) suffered in his youth a series of accidents that left him permanently disabled. It was the combination of piercing intelligence with physical deformity that created one of the most eccentric personalities of the *fin de siècle*, a man who could be intensely touching or woundingly sarcastic. Compensating for his infirmities by emancipating himself from bourgeois convention, Lautrec plunged into the nocturnal world of Paris theatres, clubs and brothels, finding there the models for his paintings, which are markedly influenced by Degas and Japanese prints. In true Baudelairian spirit, he sought beauty in degradation, and his oils, pastels and lithographs provide an exceptionally vivid picture of the world of entertainment in the late nineteenth century.

In 1895 the dancer La Goulue, formerly a celebrity of the Moulin Rouge, asked the artist to decorate a fairground booth at the Foire du Trône where she planned to present her new act. Lautrec was inspired to produce two large canvases in which he invested all his skill as a poster artist, one showing La Goulue dancing at the Moulin Rouge with her partner Valentin le Désossé, the other representing her as a Moorish dancer.

Women – whether actresses, society ladies or prostitutes – were in themselves a principal source of Lautrec's inspiration as in *La Toilette* of 1896 and the album of lithographs, *Elles*, published in the same year.

173 *H. de Toulouse-Lautrec:* La toilette, *1896*
67 × 54 (26.4 × 21.3). Bequest of Pierre Goujon, 1914

174 *H. de Toulouse-Lautrec:* Henry Samary, de la Comédie Française, dans le rôle de Raoul de Vaubert dans la comédie de J. Sandeau, 'Mademoiselle de la Seiglière' (Henry Samary Performing at the Comédie Française), *1889*
75 × 52 (29.5 × 20.5). Gift of Jacques Laroche, subject to a life interest, 1947; entered national collection 1976

173

174

175

175–176 *H. de Toulouse-*
Lautrec: La danse au Moulin-
Rouge, La Goulue et Valentin
le Désossé (Dancing at the
Moulin-Rouge, La Goulue
and Valentin le Désossé)
La danse mauresque ou La
Goulue en almée (The
Moorish Dance or La Goulue
as a Moorish Dancer)

298 × 316 (117.3 × 124.4);
285 × 307.5 (112.2 × 121).
Panels decorating La Goulue's
booth at the Foire du Trône,
1895. Acquired, in fragments,
in 1929, with the exception of
the section showing Valentin
le Désossé, given by
Monsieur Auffray, 1929;
restored 1930

The Nabis

The Nabis did not in the strict sense constitute a school; rather they were a group of painters who were friends and who between 1888 and 1900 shared a common desire to breathe new life into painting. The members of the original group were Pierre Bonnard (1867–1947), Edouard Vuillard (1868–1940), Maurice Denis (1870–1943), Ker-Xavier Roussel (1867–1944) and Paul Ranson (1864–1909), who were students together at the Académie Julian and the Ecole des Beaux-Arts, joined soon afterwards by Félix Vallotton (1865–1925), of Swiss origin, and the sculptor Aristide Maillol (1861–1944). Their hero was Gauguin, whose famous watchword 'the freedom to dare all' was passed on to them by Sérusier on the fateful day in October 1888 when he showed them his *Talisman*, painted under Gauguin's guidance. They also admired Puvis de Chavannes, Redon and Cézanne. Denis painted a *Hommage à Cézanne* (*Homage to Cézanne*), now in the Musée d'Orsay, which shows the members of the Nabi group.

The young men regarded themselves as prophets of a new painting; the Hebrew word *nabi* means 'prophet'. Admiring Japanese prints, they copied their simplified forms, flat colour and lack of depth. Thus Bonnard, dubbed by his fellows '*le nabi japonard*', treats the members of his family in his *Partie de croquet* (*The Game of Croquet*), as silhouettes standing out sharply against a background composed of a series of large decorative masses.

As a group, they wanted to get away from easel painting and therefore tended to look to the arts of décor, from theatre design to paintings for domestic interiors, a field in which their talents flourished. The Musée d'Orsay possesses five of the nine panels painted by Vuillard in 1894 for Alexandre Natanson, editor of the famous *Revue blanche*, who commissioned the sequence for his Paris flat on the avenue du Bois, now avenue Foch. In this decorative scheme, spatial depth is conveyed by a rhythmic interpenetration of planes — suggested, perhaps, by no more than the vertical of a tree-trunk or the curved outline of a clump of trees. The same rhythmic composition is apparent in Maurice Denis's modern

189 *P. Bonnard:* La partie de croquet *ou* Le crépuscule (The Game of Croquet, *or* Twilight), *1892*
130 × 162 (51.2 × 63.8). Salon des Indépendants, Paris, 1892. Gift of Daniel Wildenstein, by the agency of the Société des Amis d'Orsay, 1985

190–191 *E. Vuillard:* Jardins publics (The Park), *five of nine decorative panels executed for Alexandre Natanson, 1894*
215 × 88 (84.6 × 34.6); 215 × 92 (84.6 × 36.2); 212 × 152 (83.5 × 59.8); 212 × 80 (83.5 × 31.5); 212 × 80 (83.5 × 31.5). Left to right: Les fillettes jouant (Girls Playing), L'interrogatoire (The Interrogation), *Radot bequest, 1978;* La conversation (The Conversation), Les nourrices (Nannies), L'ombrelle rouge (The Red Parasol), *acquired 1929*

192 *F. Vallotton:* Le ballon (The Ball), *1899*
Bequest of Carle Dreyfus, 1953

193 *M. Denis:* Les muses (The Muses), *1893*
49.5 × 62 (19.5 × 24.4). Acquired 1932

190

192

193

interpretation of the mythological *Muses*, very much in the spirit of Art Nouveau with its emphasis on such decorative elements as the leaves of the chestnut trees and the generous deployment of serpentine curves.

Vallotton made eloquent use of foreshortening, influenced by his experience of wood-engraving, and conveyed a sense of space by the juxtaposition of dark and light areas, set in a rising, horizonless perspective.

It is this free handling of motifs, often accompanied by marvellously subtle distortions, this fundamentally decorative approach, that makes the Nabi movement so significant in the development of painting towards autonomy, one of the mainsprings of modern art.

194

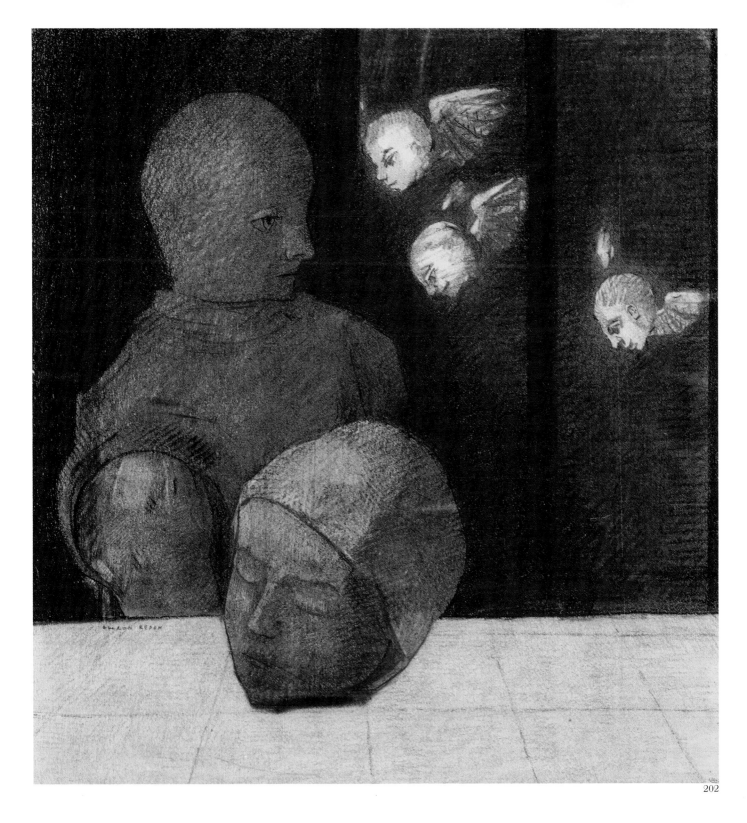

202

203

145

Photography

204

204 *J. M. Cameron:* Maud
(*illustration for* The Idylls of
the King and Other Poems *by
Tennyson, variant), 1874–75
Carbon print. 32.5 × 26.5
(12.8 × 10.4). Acquired 1985*

Spreading through advanced artistic organizations at the turn of the century – notably in the English-speaking countries – the movement towards 'art' or 'pictorialist' photography marked a decisive stage in the realization of the creative potential of the medium. It established the validity of the photographer's subjective vision and legitimized the role of imagination in photography. Pride of place is therefore given in the museum displays to this type of photography, which is closely related to the aesthetics of Art Nouveau and the paintings of the Impressionists, Symbolists and Nabis exhibited elsewhere in the collections.

It was in England, as photographers began to draw on literary and Romantic sources in the composition of their works, that the debate raged most fiercely. Could a photograph be a work of art? Could it be a picture comparable with a painting? Julia Margaret Cameron (1815–79) succeeded in revolutionizing the whole concept of portrait photography. Using purely photographic means (close-up and soft-focus) she anticipated certain effects of film in her timeless transpositions of scenes from Italian Renaissance painting. Cameron's innovations (though not her Italianate subjects) were assimilated in the work of Edward Steichen (1879–1973), one of the members of the American Photo-Secession group founded in 1902 by Alfred Stieglitz (1864–1946), himself one of the great portrait photographers. *The Kiss* by Clarence White (1871–1925), another member of the group, takes its inspiration directly from the illustrations of Aubrey Beardsley and the paintings of the Pre-Raphaelites. In contrast Stieglitz's series *City of Ambition* presents a wonderfully vivid symbolic portrait of New York. His shot of immigrants travelling steerage, of 1907 – an image admired by Picasso – marks the definitive emergence of a new photography.

205

205 *F. Evans:* The Illustrator
Aubrey Beardsley *(1872–98),
1894
Platinotype. 15 × 10
(5.9 × 3.9). Acquired 1985*

206 *C. H. White:* The Kiss,
*1899
Platinotype, gelatin treated
with bichromate. 24.7 × 14.8
(9.7 × 5.8). Gift of Société C.D.F.
Chimie Terpolymères, 1985*

207 *A. Stieglitz:* New York,
City of Ambition, *1910
Printed by photogravure on
Japan paper 1910–15.
33.7 × 25.9 (13.3 × 10.2).
Acquired 1980*

207

206

208

209

210 *E. Barrias:* La Nature se
dévoilant à la Science (Nature
Unveiling Herself to Science),
1899
*Marble, onyx, malachite, lapis
lazuli, granite. 200 (78.7).
Commissioned for
Conservatoire des Arts et
Métiers in 1899. Assigned to
national collection 1903*

211 *W. Guérin et Cie,
porcelain manufacturers in
Limoges; E. Cavaillé-Coll,
architect; M. Rouillard,
painter, decorator:*
Monumental basin
*Hard-paste porcelain, with
painted decoration. 95, d. 80
(37.4, d. 31.5). Designed 1882.
Entered national collection
1892*

212 *J. P. Aubé, sculptor;
Thiébault Frères, metal-
founders; Berquin-Varangoz,
lapidary:* La France convie la
Russie à visiter la capitale
(France Invites Russia to
View the Capital). *1899*
*Table centrepiece. Silver and
rock-crystal. 64 × 95 × 42
(25.2 × 37.4 × 16.5).
Commissioned by the state to
commemorate the visit of Tsar
Nicholas II on 6–8 October
1896*

213 *J. P. Aubé, sculptor; L. C.
Boileau, architect:* Monument
à Gambetta (Memorial to
Gambetta), *1884*
*Plaster. 240 (94.5). Winning
design in competition of 1884.
Loaned by Musée des Arts
Décoratifs, 1980*

210

The political upheavals of 1870–71 – the Franco-Prussian War, the Commune, the installation of the Third Republic – could hardly fail to find some reflection in the artistic sphere. Works directly inspired by political events were, however, slow to emerge. Even *L'énigme* (*The Enigma*) by Gustave Doré (1832–83), painted in 1871 (as were two other compositions explicitly citing the German eagle), was in fact a response to some lines written long before by Victor Hugo:

> *O Spectacle. Ainsi meurt ce que les peuples font!*
> *Qu'un tel passé pour l'âme est un gouffre profond.*

> O spectacle. Thus do the deeds of peoples die!
> How deep an abyss, for the soul, is such a past!

These particular pictures remained in the artist's studio, and were not seen in public until the posthumous auction of Doré's work.

The old styles of painting suffered scarcely a setback. Jules Lefebvre (1836–1911) was a painter in the full academic tradition, and winner of the Prix de Rome in 1861. His *Vérité* (*Truth*) was exhibited at the Salon of 1870, purchased for the nation and installed in the Musée du Luxembourg in 1874, the year of the Impressionists' first exhibition.

A few years later the state severed its links with the official Salon, handing over responsibility for the selection process to the Société des Artistes Français in 1880. And yet official art continued to flourish. The reason is not hard to seek. Lefebvre and Bouguereau, for example, were teachers at the Académie Julian. It was they, and others of the same persuasion, who formed and modelled the younger generation of artists.

The history painter Jean-Paul Laurens (1838–1921) experienced his hour of glory in the early years of the Third Republic, specializing in patriotic themes which – like *L'excommunication de Robert le Pieux* (*The Excommunication of Robert the Pious*) of 1875 – were reproduced in school textbooks.

220

220 *J. Lefebvre:* La Vérité (Truth)
265 × 112 (104.3 × 44.1). Salon of 1870. Acquired 1871

221

The younger artists were not entirely oblivious of the new Naturalism. One of the big successes of the Salon of 1880 was *Caïn* (*Cain*), an ambitious composition by Fernand Cormon (1845–1924) that dispensed entirely with the smooth-surfaced academic manner, while still being based on preparatory life drawings done in the studio in the conventional fashion. Jules Bastien-Lepage (1848–84) adopted the light palette and impulsive brushwork of Manet's young friends the Impressionists, and became the champion of the strain of 'official Naturalism' that was to take over the Salon in the years 1880–1900; much imitated outside France, this was the style that provoked vehement opposition from the Idealists and Symbolists.

221 *F. Cormon:* Caïn (Cain), *1880 (after the opening lines of 'La conscience', from* La Légende des siècles *by Victor Hugo, 1859)* *384 × 700 (115.2 × 275.6). Salon of 1880. Acquired 1880*

222 *J. Bastien-Lepage:* Les foins (Haymaking), *1877* *180 × 195 (70.9 × 76.8). Salon of 1878. Acquired 1885*

223 *E. Fremiet:* Saint Michel terrassant le dragon (St Michael Slaying the Dragon), *1879–96* *Hammered copper by the firm of Monduit, replica of the statue surmounting the spire of Mont Saint-Michel, Brittany. 617 (243). Gift of Madame G. Pasquier to Monuments historiques. Loan from Direction du patrimoine, 1980*

223

222

155

Dalou

Following the example of Courbet, Daumier and Zola, French sculpture determinedly reverted to the principles of 'Realism' – although in truth it had barely deviated from that course except under the influence of the academics. Vincenzo Vela (1820–91) in Italy and Constantin Meunier (1831–1905) in Belgium were among the innovators. They turned to their fellow men and women to find their subject matter, and dispensed with the window-dressing of historical, mythological or religious themes.

Jules Dalou (1838–1902) had played an active part in the 1870 Paris Commune and afterwards escaped to England with his family. It was from London that he submitted his design for the *Triomphe de la République* (*Triumph of the Republic*) in 1879, the year of the amnesty. *Le forgeron* (*The Blacksmith*) wears clogs and an apron as he rolls his cartwheel, and carries his hammer slung over his shoulder; no one could mistake him for Vulcan. Indeed, he was destined to be the central figure in a *Monument au travail* (*Monument to Labour*) that was never constructed.

Dalou's terracotta studies are rooted in the observation of life. His nude study for the *Republic* shows a body with weaknesses as well as strengths; it is clear that it represents a real woman and only secondarily an allegorical figure.

224

225

239

238

240

Aspects of painting
outside France

Painting outside France in the 1880s and 1890s was largely dominated by different schools of Realism, often variants and extensions of movements in French painting such as Impressionism and Neo-Impressionism (Divisionism). In the last ten years of the century there was a trend towards Symbolism, variously interpreted in the different countries.

La dame en détresse (*The Lady in Distress*) of 1882 belongs to the early period of the Belgian painter James Ensor (1860–1949). He was influenced initially by Impressionism, but in the 1880s moved on to more domestic themes, following the *intimiste* paintings of artists like Bonnard and Vuillard. Later still, his canvases reflected an interest in the unconscious, becoming increasingly Symbolist in character, representing masks and grotesque figures that are in a direct line of descent from Hieronymus Bosch.

In Italy around 1892–95, Giuseppe Pellizza da Volpedo (1868–1907) adopted a technique derived from French Neo-Impressionism, as did Vittore Grubicy di Drago, Angelo Morbelli and – outstandingly – Giovanni Segantini. Pellizza drew extensively on social and humanitarian themes, but a work such as *Fleur brisée (Broken Blossom)*, *c.*1896–1902, demonstrates that he also understood the vocabulary of Symbolism.

Of a different order altogether is the Symbolism of the Belgian painter Léon Frédéric (1896–1940). His great triptych *Les âges de l'ouvrier (The Ages of the Working Man)* is a celebration of manual labour in a style verging almost on Hyper-Realism, belonging to the same vein of social Symbolism as the contemporary works of his compatriots Constantin Meunier and Eugène Laermans.

One of the dominant figures in American painting was the Bostonian Winslow Homer (1836–1910), who discovered Impressionism when he visited Paris. His love of the sea is reflected in his *Summer Night*, a mysterious and resonant painting of great evocative power.

Rodin

A large area of the terraces on the first floor is given up to Auguste Rodin (1840–1917) and the group of young sculptors who worked with him as assistants: Jules Desbois (1851–1935), Lucien Schnegg (1864–1909), Antoine Bourdelle (1861–1929), and Camille Claudel (1864–1943), whose masterpiece *L'âge mûr* (*Maturity*), inspired by the ending of her relationship with Rodin, is shown together with the latter's sculptures.

The Musée d'Orsay is particularly fortunate in having in its possession four large plaster casts on permanent loan from the Musée Rodin. It is thus possible to trace Rodin's development from *L'âge d'airain* (*The Bronze Age*), with its naturalistic modelling, right through to the *Muse Whistler* (*Muse or Monument to Whistler*), handled with such freedom that it amounts to little more than a number of loosely related elements, linked together by a piece of draped cloth dipped in plaster.

During the 1880s Rodin's major project was *La porte de l'Enfer* (*The Gate of Hell*) commissioned for the nation in 1880 and changed only in minor details after 1890, and also to

245 *A. Rodin:* La Porte de l'enfer (The Gate of Hell), *1880–1917*
Plaster. 635 (245). Loan from Musée Rodin, 1986

246 *C. Claudel:* L'âge mur (The Age of Maturity), *1894–1903*
Bronze. 114 (44.9). 1982

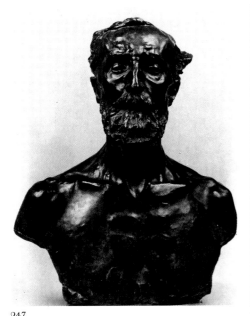

247

248

249

247　*A. Rodin:* A. J. Dalou
*(1838–1902), sculptor, 1884
Bronze. 54.5 (21.5). Acquired
1907*

248　*A. Rodin:* Madame
Vicuña, *1888
Marble. 57 (22.4). Acquired
1888*

249　*A. Rodin:* La Pensée
(Thought), *c. 1886–89
Marble. 74 (29.1). Gift of
Mme Durand who had bought
it from Rodin for the Musée
du Luxembourg, 1902*

250　*A. Rodin: Balzac, 1898
Plaster. 300 (118). Loan from
Musée Rodin, 1986. The
photograph by Steichen was
given to the Musée d'Orsay by
A.S.D.A., 1981. 20.3 × 15.6
(8 × 6.1)*

a series of portrait busts. Both the *Gate of Hell* and the bust of
Dalou reveal Rodin's admiration for the Italian Renaissance,
the former being inspired by Dante's *Divine Comedy.* Amid
the tangle of bodies condemned by passion to the abyss, two
principal episodes are represented: on the left, Paolo and
Francesca locked in embrace (the origin of the famous *Baiser,
The Kiss*), and on the right, the figures of Ugolino and his
children (of which the exhibit in the Musée d'Orsay is a
larger-scale copy). The *Gate of Hell* was too large to be
worked in one piece of clay and was therefore modelled in
sections, each of which exists as a separate sculpture: *Le
Penseur* (*The Thinker*), *Fugit Amor, Ombres* (*The Shades*),
etc.

Ultimately Rodin was to move increasingly in the
direction of abstraction, as in *La pensée* (*Thought*) – which
echoes another powerful image of human creativity, the bust
of *Goethe* by Pierre Jean David d'Angers, situated in the
entrance-hall of the museum – and, to outstanding effect, in
his statue of *Balzac.* The change in his style can be measured
by the progress from those early nude studies of visionary
Realism, which become increasingly more simplified and
distorted ('in my view, modern sculpture should exaggerate
the forms to express mental attributes'), arriving finally at
this pyramidal silhouette, the emphasis all on the large head.
This almost abstract symbol of the novelist's powers aroused
such a furore when it was shown to the public in 1898 that the
commission was withdrawn. Today it is recognized as Rodin's
most innovatory sculpture.

251 *G. Serrurier-Bovy:* Bed,
c. *1898–99*
Mahogany, brass fittings.
280 × 210 × 240
(110.2 × 82.7 × 94.5). Acquired
1984 with complete set of
bedroom furnishings including
two wardrobes, dressing-table
and cheval-glass

251

279

wrote of it: 'The extraordinary exaggerated stance of the archer poised in space ... that human form which seems to surge forward even in immobility, that incisive and accurate modelling, so full and vibrant; it is one of the most prodigious efforts of contemporary art.'

Whereas Gauguin and Lacombe – and Maillol in his early years – had carved almost exclusively in wood, Joseph Bernard (1866–1931) adopted the practice of direct carving in stone. His *Effort vers la nature* (*Towards Nature*) suggests, both by its title and its massive, primitive appearance, a desire for close harmony between form and matter; it was the prelude to works carved directly out of huge blocks of stone, in the manner that was to be adopted by Henry Moore, Amedeo Modigliani, Jacob Epstein and Constantin Brancusi. Bernard's figures are more supple and rhythmic than Maillol's, with a spirituality reflecting the artist's own mysticism. A particularly fine example is the *Porteuse d'eau* (*Water Carrier*) of 1912.

278 *J. Bernard:* Effort vers la nature (Towards Nature), c. *1906–07*
Stone, directly carved. 32 (12.6). Gift of Jean Bernard, 1980

279 *E. A. Bourdelle:* Heraklès archer (Heracles the Bowman), *1909*
Bronze. 248 (97.6). Acquired 1924

280

186

286

287

288 *L. Spilliaert:* Clair de lune et lumières (Moonlight and Lamps), c. *1909*
Indian ink wash and pastel. 65 × 50 (25.6 × 19.7). Gift of Mme Madeleine Spilliaert, the artist's daughter, 1981

289 *J. Toorop:* Le Désir et l'Assouvissement (Desire and Fulfilment), *1893*
Pastel on beige paper. 76 × 90 (29.9 × 35.4). Acquired 1976

288

289

Drawing and watercolour

The Nabis were enthusiastic practitioners of all the graphic arts – prints, posters, book illustrations, etc. – and between them produced a vast quantity of drawings, those by Bonnard being probably the finest and most attractive. His wide-ranging imagination is evident both in rapid sketches and more finished pastels and watercolours. Théophile Steinlen (1859–1923), in a more down-to-earth spirit, presents us with a vivid picture of his times. The major collection of works by Cappiello reflects the revival of poster art, also represented by Jules Chéret (1836-1932) and Toulouse-Lautrec. The Symbolists too, like Gustave Moreau, were prolific draughtsmen: the drawings of Lévy-Dhurmer or Carlos Schwabe, for example, are of particular appeal to contemporary taste. As in a similar vein, although different in mood, are the works of the Italian Segantini, the Belgian Léon Spilliaert (1881–1946), and the Dutchman Jan Toorop (1858–1928), which – like the major series by Alfons Mucha (1860–1939), linked to Art Nouveau – are recent additions to the collections.

290

290 *A. Mucha:* Plate for 'Documents décoratifs' *Crayon and white gouache on beige card. 54.4 × 40.5 (21.4 × 15.9). Gift of Jiři Mucha, 1979*

291 *P. Bonnard:* Project for an Interior (detail) *Pen and watercolour. 50.2 × 35.6 (19.8 × 14) overall. Gift of Mlles Alice and Marguerite Bowers, 1984*

291

Music at the
Musée d'Orsay

The museum's coverage of the arts from 1848 to 1914 would be incomplete without reference to the music of the period, which is represented in a number of exhibitions and in an ambitious programme of concerts.

Musical activities are catered for in a number of attractive settings. The main auditorium, with seating for 385, will be the venue for evenings of chamber music, covering the major European works of the period and also less well-known works that merit revival. The seasons are planned in such a way that it will, over a period, be possible to hear the entire repertoire of chamber and piano works by, for example, Brahms, Schumann, Debussy, Fauré or Ravel.

The *Salle des Fêtes* of the Palais d'Orsay has been restored and now houses sculptures of the Third Republic. It provides a perfect setting for recreating the atmosphere of turn-of-the-century-bourgeois salon-life, and will be used for shorter recitals in a lighter vein, held in the late afternoon. Some of these programmes will be repeated in the auditorium, at lunch-times, aimed primarily at the many people who work in the area. Music also plays a part in the activities provided for the young; the history of music is one of the themes of the programme of lectures and seminars. Selections of light music will be a regular feature in the renovated restaurant, and it is intended to revive the tradition of café music at tea-time on Sunday afternoons.

On special occasions the great nave of the museum will house large-scale concert performances of the major symphonic and choral works of the latter half of the nineteenth century.

Finally, it is intended to make available to the public a selection of recordings, both reissues of historic performances and live recordings of concerts of rarely performed works. Many of the concerts are to be broadcast by Radio-France, enabling the musical activities of the Musée d'Orsay to reach a wider public in France and abroad.

296

296 *E. Degas:* L'orchestre de
l'Opéra (The Opéra
Orchestra), *c. 1868–69*
56.5 × 46 (22.2 × 18.1). In the
foreground is Désiré Dihau,
bassoonist and friend of
Degas; in the box is the

composer Emanuel Chabrier
who was a great collector of
Manet and the Impressionists.
Acquired from Marie Dihau,
the sitter's sister, subject to a
life interest, 1924; entered
national collection 1935

Literature at the Musée d'Orsay

The year 1848 saw the publication of the first volume of François-René de Chateaubriand's *Mémoires d'Outre-Tombe*; 1913 that of the first volume of Marcel Proust's *A la Recherche du temps perdu*. A world separates them. Chateaubriand records the history of the first half of the century, from Revolution to Romanticism, while Proust's great fictional sequence looks ahead to the modern novel, as exemplified by Joyce, Musil or Faulkner. It is impossible to outline in a few words the literary history of a period of such upheaval, full of trends and counter-trends, schools and factions, and individual acts of iconoclasm – a period, too, in which new links were forged between literature and the press. If one were to attempt to sum up the spirit of the age – that drive towards modernity exhibited in so much of the writing of the time – it would be necessary to look beyond France itself. For this was a European impulse, manifested as much in London, Vienna or Prague as in Paris. Inevitably, however, our principal concern here must be with French writers.

With the benefit of hindsight, it is possible to establish a progression from Baudelaire to Arthur Rimbaud (1854–91), who wrote in 'Le bateau ivre', 'I regret the passing of Europe with its ancient parapets'; or, equally, from Stéphane Mallarmé (1842–98) through to Guillaume Apollinaire (1880–1918), who began his poem 'Zone', the first in the sequence *Alcools* (1913), with these words: 'In the end you tire of this ancient world'. 'Zone' is both a poetic manifesto and an exhortation to start afresh – appallingly ironic in view of the long and bloody war that followed.

One undeniable feature of literature in the period 1848–1914 was its pessimism, particularly marked in the novels of the period. Gustave Flaubert (1821–80) acidly dispels any last shreds of romantic illusion; Victor Hugo (1802–85) tears apart the classical narrative tradition, left untouched by Stendhal (1783–1842) and Honoré de Balzac (1799–1850), and attacks conformity with a bitterness born of despair. *Germinal* by Emile Zola (1840–1902) is a chronicle of disaster, despite its author's belief in work and progress; the Naturalism of J.K. Huysmans (1848–1907) dwindles into decadent aestheticism, taking refuge finally in mysticism. Ultimately it was Proust who painted on a vast canvas the picture of a society whose foundations were crumbling, a pathetic ruin standing on the brink of a new century. It is ironic that these years, from 1830 to 1914, saw the finest flowering of the French novel. It is almost as though the writers sensed a new era in the making, as though their creative powers were stimulated by the discontent and unease provoked in them by the awareness that their society was in crisis.

The period was also characterized by the close relationship that developed between art and literature – a phenomenon recorded in the press, in books and later in films. Great writers were also painters, great painters published books. Victor Hugo was one of the best graphic artists the century produced; Eugène Fromentin (1820–76) was as much a writer as he was a painter; Théophile Gautier (1811–72) and Baudelaire both sketched; and we turn to Delacroix's *Journal*, or the writings of Gauguin or Van Gogh, with a pleasure that derives as much from their value as literature as from their relevance as art-historical documents.

Following in the tradition of Diderot and Stendhal, writers such as Baudelaire, Octave Mirbeau (1850–1917), Zola and Mallarmé were also self-appointed art critics, often publishing their reviews of the Salons and other articles alongside the writings of professional journalists, in reviews such as *L'Artiste* or *La Revue Blanche* – to which the painters and engravers themselves also contributed.

The movements of Romanticism, Realism and Symbolism were common to painting and literature. Inter-relationships between the practitioners bore unexpected fruits: Baudelaire's passion for Delacroix and for Wagner, for example, had a profound influence on his poetry. The brief period of Symbolist dominance brought together all the arts in an unprecedented unity.

Art became one of the principal topics discussed in literature. Novels were full of painters and paintings: Gustave Moreau lives again through the pages of Huysmans' *A Rebours*, and Cézanne haunts Zola's *L'Oeuvre*. In Proust's *A la Recherche du temps perdu*, Elstir, Vinteuil and La Berma are the synthesis of all the painters, musicians and artists of the turn of the century.

Thus literature, too, has its place in the Musée d'Orsay. It will be discussed in debates and lectures, in terms of its relationship to art and history; it will even feature – somewhat paradoxically one might think – in exhibitions, displayed on the walls together with the paintings (though that will seem less strange if one refers to Pierre Larousse's *Grand Dictionnaire Universel du XIXème siècle* and reads its astonishing definition of a museum: '… *fig:* Collection, assembly for the purposes of study. A dictionary, with its many examples, is a *Museum*').

Hugo once likened 'cathedrals of paper' to cathedrals of stone: both are monuments, both endure.

297 *E. Manet:* Stéphane Mallarmé *(1842–98), poet, 1876.*
27.5 × 36 (10.8 × 14.2).
Acquired 1928 with the assistance of the Société des Amis du Louvre and D. David-Weill.

Index

Numbers in *italic* refer to the illustrations.

Photo credits

Réunion des musées nationaux (D. Arnaudet, G. Blot, C. Jean, J. Schormans)
and Musée d'Orsay (Jim Purcell)
with the exception of the following:
Fonds Urphot (pp 10, 11)
Bibliothèque nationale (195, 196, 198, 199)
Cliché musée de Roubaix (215)
Cinémathèque française (295)
Lyon, coll. Institut Lumière (294)